The Political Anthropology of Ethnic and Religious Minorities

This book presents some arguments for why a political anthropological perspective can be particularly helpful for understanding the connected political and cultural challenges and opportunities posed by the situation of ethnic and religious minorities. The first chapter shortly introduces the major anthropological concepts used, including liminality, trickster, imitation, and schismogenesis; concepts that are used together with approaches of historical sociology and genealogy, especially concerning the rise and fall of empires, and their lasting impact. The conceptual framework suggested here is particularly helpful for understanding how marginal places can become liminal, appearing suddenly at the center of political attention. The introduction also shows the manner in which minority existence can problematize the depersonalizing tendencies of modern globalization. Subsequent chapters demonstrate how the political anthropological conceptual framework presented can be used for various European regions, through the cases of certain ethnic and religious minorities, and each illustrates that instead of charismatic leaders, trickster politicians are emerging and increasingly dominate, through the "public sphere," the space of modern politics emptied of real presence.

The chapters in this book were originally published as a special issue of *Nationalism and Ethnic Politics*.

Arpad Szakolczai is Professor of Sociology at University College Cork, Ireland, and has previously taught at the European University Institute, Florence, Italy. His recent books include *Comedy and the Public Sphere: The Rebirth of Theatre as Comedy and the Genealogy of the Modern Public Arena* (2013), *Novels and the Sociology of the Contemporary* (2016), and *Permanent Liminality and Modernity: Analysing the Sacrificial Carnival through Novels* (2017).

Agnes Horvath is a sociologist and political scientist with an interest in an anthropological understanding of modernity. She has taught in Hungary, Italy, and Ireland. Her publications include *Walking into the Void: A Historical Sociology and Political Anthropology of Walking* (2018), *Modernism and Charisma* (2013), and *Breaking Boundaries: Varieties of Liminality* (2015).

Attila Z. Papp is a sociologist, and he is director of the Institute for Minority Studies at the Hungarian Academy of Sciences, Centre for Social Sciences, Budapest, Hungary. His articles include *21st Century Hungarian Language Survival in Transylvania* (2015) and *Minority Hungarian Communities in the Twentieth Century* (2010).

The Political Anthropology of Ethnic and Religious Minorities

Edited by
Arpad Szakolczai, Agnes Horvath and Attila Z. Papp

LONDON AND NEW YORK

First published 2018
by Routledge
2 Park Square, Milton Park, Abingdon, Oxon, OX14 4RN, UK

and by Routledge
711 Third Avenue, New York, NY 10017, USA

Routledge is an imprint of the Taylor & Francis Group, an informa business

© 2018 Taylor & Francis

All rights reserved. No part of this book may be reprinted or reproduced or utilised in any form or by any electronic, mechanical, or other means, now known or hereafter invented, including photocopying and recording, or in any information storage or retrieval system, without permission in writing from the publishers.

Trademark notice: Product or corporate names may be trademarks or registered trademarks, and are used only for identification and explanation without intent to infringe.

British Library Cataloguing in Publication Data
A catalogue record for this book is available from the British Library

ISBN 13: 978-0-8153-8212-6

Typeset in Garamond
by diacriTech, Chennai

Publisher's Note
The publisher accepts responsibility for any inconsistencies that may have arisen during the conversion of this book from journal articles to book chapters, namely the possible inclusion of journal terminology.

Disclaimer
Every effort has been made to contact copyright holders for their permission to reprint material in this book. The publishers would be grateful to hear from any copyright holder who is not here acknowledged and will undertake to rectify any errors or omissions in future editions of this book.

Contents

Citation Information		vii
Notes on Contributors		ix
1	Individualization as Depersonalization: Minority Studies and Political Anthropology *Arpad Szakolczai, Agnes Horvath, and Attila Z. Papp*	1
2	Trickster Logics in the Hungarian Dual-Citizenship Offer *Attila Z. Papp*	18
3	"Liminal" Orthodoxies on the Margins of Empire: Twentieth-Century "Home-Grown" Religious Movements in the Republic of Moldova *James Kapaló*	33
4	Fluid Identity, Fluid Citizenship: The Problem of Ethnicity in Postcommunist Romania *Marius Ion Benţa*	52
5	Central Marginality: Minorities, Images, and Victimhood in Central-Eastern Europe *Arvydas Grišinas*	66
6	Defending the Nation from her Nationalism(s) *Jesenko Tešan*	81
7	Reconciliation and After in Northern Ireland: The Search for a Political Order in an Ethnically Divided Society *Duncan Morrow*	98
8	"In the Margins of Europe": Cypriot Nationalism, Liminality, and the Moral Economy of the Financial Crisis *Vassos Argyrou*	118
Index		133

Citation Information

The chapters in this book were originally published in *Nationalism and Ethnic Politics*, volume 23, issue 1 (2017). When citing this material, please use the original page numbering for each article, as follows:

Chapter 1
Individualization as Depersonalization: Minority Studies and Political Anthropology
Arpad Szakolczai, Agnes Horvath, and Attila Z. Papp
Nationalism and Ethnic Politics, volume 23, issue 1 (2017) pp. 1–17

Chapter 2
Trickster Logics in the Hungarian Dual-Citizenship Offer
Attila Z. Papp
Nationalism and Ethnic Politics, volume 23, issue 1 (2017) pp. 18–32

Chapter 3
"Liminal" Orthodoxies on the Margins of Empire: Twentieth-Century "Home-Grown" Religious Movements in the Republic of Moldova
James Kapaló
Nationalism and Ethnic Politics, volume 23, issue 1 (2017) pp. 33–51

Chapter 4
Fluid Identity, Fluid Citizenship: The Problem of Ethnicity in Postcommunist Romania
Marius Ion Benţa
Nationalism and Ethnic Politics, volume 23, issue 1 (2017) pp. 52–65

Chapter 5
Central Marginality: Minorities, Images, and Victimhood in Central-Eastern Europe
Arvydas Grišinas
Nationalism and Ethnic Politics, volume 23, issue 1 (2017) pp. 66–80

CITATION INFORMATION

Chapter 6
Defending the Nation from her Nationalism(s)
Jesenko Tešan
Nationalism and Ethnic Politics, volume 23, issue 1 (2017) pp. 81–97

Chapter 7
Reconciliation and After in Northern Ireland: The Search for a Political Order in an Ethnically Divided Society
Duncan Morrow
Nationalism and Ethnic Politics, volume 23, issue 1 (2017) pp. 98–117

Chapter 8
"In the Margins of Europe": Cypriot Nationalism, Liminality, and the Moral Economy of the Financial Crisis
Vassos Argyrou
Nationalism and Ethnic Politics, volume 23, issue 1 (2017) pp. 118–132

For any permission-related enquiries please visit:
http://www.tandfonline.com/page/help/permissions

Notes on Contributors

Vassos Argyrou is professor of Social Anthropology and Cultural Theory at the University of Hull, UK. His latest book is *The Gift of European Thought and the Cost of Living* (Berghahn, 2013).

Marius Ion Benţa is Guest Lecturer in the Department of Journalism at the Babeş-Bolyai University, Cluj-Napoca, Romania, and a journalist. His main research interests are phenomenological sociology, social theory, identity, media, and technology. His book *Experiencing Multiple Realities* is forthcoming with Routledge, 2018.

Arvydas Grišinas is a Lecturer at the Vilnius Academy of Arts, Lithuania. His research interests include political anthropology, experiential history, and identity formation (particularly in Central-Eastern Europe). His book *Politics with a Human Face* is forthcoming with Routledge, 2018.

Agnes Horvath is a sociologist and political scientist with an interest in an anthropological understanding of modernity. She has taught in Hungary, Italy, and Ireland. Her publications include *Walking into the Void: A Historical Sociology and Political Anthropology of Walking* (2018), *Modernism and Charisma* (2013), and *Breaking Boundaries: Varieties of Liminality* (2015).

James Kapaló is Senior Lecturer in the Study of Religions at University College Cork, Ireland. His research interests are minority religions in Eastern and Central Europe, folk and material religion, and religions in the secret police archives in postcommunist states. He is Principal Investigator of the European Research Council funded project *Creative Agency and Religious Minorities: Hidden Galleries in the Secret Police Archives in Central and Eastern Europe*.

Duncan Morrow is lecturer in Politics at Ulster University, Coleraine, UK, where he is also Director of Community Engagement. Previously, he was CEO of the Northern Ireland Community Relations Council, where he championed the concept of a shared future and peace-building through community practice, public policy, research, and active learning.

NOTES ON CONTRIBUTORS

Attila Z. Papp is a sociologist, and he is director of the Institute for Minority Studies at the Hungarian Academy of Sciences, Centre for Social Sciences, Budapest, Hungary. His articles include *21st Century Hungarian Language Survival in Transylvania* (2015) and *Minority Hungarian Communities in the Twentieth Century* (2010).

Arpad Szakolczai is Professor of Sociology at University College Cork, Ireland, and has previously taught at the European University Institute, Florence, Italy. His recent books include *Comedy and the Public Sphere: The Rebirth of Theatre as Comedy and the Genealogy of the Modern Public Arena* (2013), *Novels and the Sociology of the Contemporary* (2016), and *Permanent Liminality and Modernity: Analysing the Sacrificial Carnival through Novels* (2017).

Jesenko Tešan is a doctoral candidate at the Department of Sociology, University College Cork, Ireland.

Individualization as Depersonalization: Minority Studies and Political Anthropology

ARPAD SZAKOLCZAI and AGNES HORVATH

ATTILA Z. PAPP

This chapter offers an introduction to the book. It presents the arguments why a political anthropological perspective can be particularly helpful to understand the connected political and cultural challenges and opportunities posed by the situation of ethnic and religious minorities. The article concisely introduces the major anthropological concepts used, including liminality, trickster, imitation, and schismogenesis; concepts that are used together with approaches of historical sociology and genealogy, especially concerning the rise and fall of empires, and their lasting impact. The suggested conceptual framework is particularly helpful for understanding how marginal places can become liminal, appearing suddenly at the center of political attention. The article also shows the manner in which minority existence can problematize the depersonalizing tendencies of modern globalization.

There are, at least, five good reasons why minorities—ethnic, linguistic, or religious—are a worthwhile, even important, area of study for the political and social sciences. To begin with, and most simply, because they simply *exist*, even though often they are ignored, or belittled, following the seemingly self-evident logic of identifying a nation-state with a single group. Second, such groups offer *color* and *variety*; it is *good* to know about them, as they help to stay aware about the multiplicity of life and culture in a world increasingly threatened by global uniformity. Third, and even more importantly, beyond "exotic" charm, such communities offer a reality check against these processes of mechanization and uniformization, moving beyond the idea of taking the "modern West" as an unsurpassable horizon. Fourth, beyond merely surviving, in contrast to the dominant majority of their respective countries, they perform, or could perform, an important role of mediation. Fifth and perhaps most importantly, the existence of such minorities both render evident and help to literally resist the arguably most central and most pernicious aspects of modern globalization, which is not simply standardization, mechanization, bureaucratization, commodification, or commercialization but also *depersonalization*. The central aim is to analyze this phenomenon with the help of concepts developed in political anthropology.

This short introduction will offer an overview of political anthropology,[1] with a focus on its features that might have particular relevance for minority studies. The central aim of this volume is to suggest a theoretical framework for analyzing the situation and role of minorities, with a focus on deeply divided societies, and to apply it for some European countries where significant ethnic minorities are present, and where there is a strong religion-based conflict dividing the society. Anthropological concepts central for this theoretical framework include liminality, imitation, trickster, and schismogenesis; concepts that are little used, especially together, outside specialized anthropological studies but that have particular relevance for the study of sociopolitical conflicts in the modern world. In particular, using the conceptual pair "marginality/liminality," this volume investigates how such situations emerge in peripheral areas that are also in between major cultural, political, and civilizational centers and in the outskirts of Europe, and how such "marginal" places can gain a liminal position in mediating between societies and cultures but also in becoming permanent sources of conflict. Such at once marginal and liminal areas, studied in some details in the chapters that follow, include Hungary, Romania, Moldavia, Lithuania, Bosnia, Cyprus, and Northern Ireland.

The reason why we offer a set of anthropological concepts that were so far rarely used in the study of contemporary politics is dual, justifying the undertaking from two angles. On the one hand, living as member of a minority — ethnic, linguistic, or religious — is a matter of everyday living and an often quite difficult, conflictual one. Studies of such situations easily require the standard anthropological or ethnographic tools of extended fieldwork and participatory observation. However, on the other hand, the very existence of such minorities *as* minorities, often quite isolated and embittered minorities, is a consequence of long-term historical changes, mostly due to the building and collapse of empires. This implies, at a first step, the rise of a conquering empire, and its subjugation of various people, often involving forced population movements and then a protracted existence under such an empire that often can extend for long centuries, under which various efforts are made by central authorities to integrate and assimilate the conquered; eventually, the *necessary* collapse of an empire might lead to situations of nation-state-building with its own homogenizing efforts as a legacy. This also implies that the perspective of political anthropology makes use of comparative historical sociology, especially the genealogical perspective, as pioneered by Nietzsche and developed further by Max Weber, Eric Voegelin, and Michel Foucault.

The paradoxicality of such a situation is not always understood in contemporary political analysis. The reason is that the central concepts of modern social and political theorizing are closely connected to the specific answer given to the concrete political and religious problems that emerged in Europe after the collapse of the Byzantine Empire and *thus* the medieval world order, but theorists fail to see the contingency of their own answers, starting with the ideas of Machiavelli and More, and especially Hobbes. The significance of anthropological approaches and concepts is thus not simply that they stay close to the everyday reality of minorities but that such concepts can escape the limits of taken-for-granted modern concepts, closely tied to the (absolutist) state.

The central paradox of the postimperial situation is that the mess generated by empire-building, this "concupiscential conquest" (Voegelin), always driven by an inner void, is not easy to clear away.[2] Populations that became mixed, as forced to live together for long decades or centuries, cannot be easily separated. The oldest example for the absurdity of such efforts takes us back to the Book of Ezra in the Old Testament, a first case for ethnic cleansing, where the high priests, back — eventually — from the Babylonian captivity, stood judgment over their people, expelling those with foreign wives. In such a context, enforced homogenization by the "liberated" people can be even more oppressive and violent than imperial policies; while the seemingly "liberal" and "democratic" solution of tying down people, in a setting where intermarriage was the fact of life since generations, to a single and unambiguous ethnic identity can be just as oppressive and even ludicrous.

Beyond these problems, we would like to single out for attention one particularly problematic element of the taken-for-granted framework of modern European thought, associated with the legal, administrative, bureaucratic, processual, and policy-obsessed aspects of state formation. This is the increased *depersonalization* associated with the rise of the modern world — not exclusive to politics, but particularly pronounced there, and rendered visible by various minorities.

DEPERSONALIZATION VERSUS THE MINORITY PERSON

The problem of the depersonalizing effects of the modern state and modern capitalism was at the heart of Max Weber's work. This aspect, which cannot be reduced to the more specific diagnoses of "bureaucratization" or "rationalization," has recently been emphasized by Wilhelm Hennis, a political scientist who argued that Max Weber's central theme of work was concerned with the tension between personality and the "life orders" under contemporary conditions.[3] It is due to perceiving such depersonalizing effects that Weber was intrigued by Nietzsche's diagnosis of modern nihilism, animating some of his last conclusive words, like the January 1919 lecture *Politics as a Vocation*, containing the passage "Not summer's bloom lies ahead of us, but rather a polar night of icy darkness and hardness ... [w]here there is nothing,"[4] giving a negative response to the still open ending of the *Protestant Ethic*, envisioning that the "last men" of this civilizational development could be " 'specialists without spirit, sensualists without heart: this nullity imagines that it has attained a level of civilization never before achieved,'"[5] or his last completed lecture course on *General Economic History* in the 1919–20 winter term, ending with evoking a new "Iron Age."[6]

Such diagnoses are notable not simply due to their pessimism but by capturing a type of development where depersonalization is continually increasing, paradoxically together with rising individualism and fake personalization. This is because the term "individual" has two radically different shades of meaning. On the one hand, the "individual" stands for the concrete, single human being, implying the myriad ties and connections one carries within his or her person — family, friends, and colleagues or religious, ethnic, linguistic, and professional. On the other, in both modern economics *and* the "public sphere," the individual is a single, atomized entity, alchemically separated from every possible tie, left with nothing else but one's "interests" (a word itself capturing in-between-ness but here transmogrified into something objectified "inside" the individual) and reasoning power; thus, a conceptualization perfectly compatible with the most extreme depersonalization. Depersonalization divides entities, where each divided entity must construct an "identity" that would then be "recognized" by the others; quite close to the analogy of the way the nation-states "recognize" each other, in the Westphalian system. However, the multiplication of recognized identities does not necessarily mean an undisturbed personality but quite the opposite. Over time the negative aspects of depersonalization and the deep-seated anxieties it produces are also becoming more and more evident and dominant, leading to increasing warfare and conflicts, not only in the past but the present as well.

Thus, beyond terms like "ambivalence" or even "tension," we need concepts that can capture together both sides of modernity, depersonalization, and individualization and the increasing gap and tension between the "person" (the authentic, concrete self) and the "individual" (a bundle of sensation that tries to maximize pleasure and minimize pain, "constructing" one's identity). There is an anthropologically derived term that does this feat, and this is "bipolarity," developed by Gregory Bateson on the basis of his earlier concept of "schismogenesis." Here, we immediately enter at the heart of the history of the long past centuries, the schismatic history of the civilization to which we belong. Such schisms include the Great Schism between eastern and western Christianity, the Reformation and the subsequent further schisms within western Christianity, the schisms between nations and social classes, resulting in the social and national problems tearing apart the continent and leading to World War I, the East–West schism of the Cold War, and, most recently, the waves of mass migrations that became a new state of normalcy in the contemporary world.

By pursuing Weber's diagnosis one of the central anthropological concepts has already been introduced. In the next sections, a more systematic introduction will be offered about the central anthropological concepts on which this book relies.

POLITICAL ANTHROPOLOGY

The idea that social theory needs not only a historical but also an anthropological dimension goes back to the classics. Weber tried to incorporate anthropological studies into his approach, while Emile Durkheim, his contemporary, directly championed an anthropological perspective to sociology. However, the most relevant anthropological ideas do not derive from Durkheimian sociology but rather from its main dissenters. These include Arnold van Gennep, who in his *Rites de passage* introduced the idea "liminality," Gabriel Tarde, who suggested the centrality of the term "imitation," thus redirecting sociology to Platonic foundation, close to the ideas of Alexis de Tocqueville, and even Marcel Mauss, Durkheim's nephew and designated heir, whose ideas about the importance of praying (theme of his unfinished dissertation) and gift relations directly challenged the Durkheimian focus on rituals of sacrifice, or Lucien Lévy-Bruhl and his focus of participation, away from Durkheim's neo-Kantian concept "collective representations." Further ideas that were for a long time marginal even for anthropology but now are increasingly becoming central, through political anthropology, for social and political analysis include the "trickster" and "schismogenesis."[7]

Within the scope and limits of this writing, it is not possible to introduce these various ideas in detail. We can only illustrate how they all hang together. This offers a novel way to analyze the genesis of the modern world in depersonalization, through a series of concepts that were developed by anthropologists in their studies of nonmodern and non-Western societies. It thus overcomes the central problem of self-referentiality in social theory: analyzing the rise and dynamics of modern societies in emptying entities by concepts developed from within these same societies.

To start with, liminality helps to capture and analyze, with a degree of analytical rigor, what happens under ephemeral and fluid conditions of transition and uncertainty.[8] Rites of passage are those rituals that assist the transition of a group of individuals, or an entire community, through major points of passage in life: birth and death, adulthood and marriage, illness or other types of crises, or simply the rhythm of seasons. They have three phases: rites of separation; the rite itself, a performance or testing; and the rites of reaggregation. The main liminal moment is the middle stage, but each of the three phases is liminal in its own way.

While the concept was developed through studying rituals actually staged in various small-scale populations in the world, its relevance for the modern world, or for understanding the dynamics of historical events, is evident. A social, political, or economic crisis can be analyzed as a real-world large-scale moment of transition in which the taken-for-granted, stable structures of social and human life are suddenly suspended, and there is an intense search for a solution. This is the type of situation that was at the center of Max Weber's political sociology, the problem of an "out-of-ordinary" (*ausseralltägliche*) situation, for which he developed the term "charisma." For Weber, out-of-ordinary situations cannot be solved by ordinary, traditional-customary, or rational-legalistic means, because the stability that is the basis of such solutions was undermined. They require the appearance of a special kind of person who has "charisma" or a transcendental power for transformation. Weber clearly intimated that Europe after WWI required such leaders, but there are never guarantees that such persons would arrive.

Political sociologists and political scientists over the past century meticulously applied the Weberian terminology to the actual "out-of-ordinary" political leaders of the past century, without paying attention to the question whether these leaders had genuine charismatic qualities. This is where the anthropological concept "trickster," invented by Paul Radin, is particularly helpful.[9] Tricksters abound in folktales, mythologies, and ethnographic accounts in most cultures of the planet. The trickster is a peculiar in-between figure, specialized in soul fetching or depersonalization. It is the eternal outsider, not member of any community, not participating, thus not having emotional ties, but for the very same reason able to perceive how it is possible to direct others through their emotions, or even outright stimulate or produce emotions in others, literally playing with human emotions as if on a musical instrument. They are lonely wanderers, moving from one place to another, always in search of conditions where they could suddenly jump from the periphery into the center, making themselves useful, even indispensable, convincing people to accept the changes in themselves. Thus, tricksters are living paradoxes, both outcasts and culture heroes, in many cultures even considered as second founders of the world. The trickster is a central conceptual tool complementing Weber's "charisma" in capturing a type of political leader that is outside both the realm of tradition and legal rationality. The conditions that favor their rise are situations of distress or crisis, where stabilities are dissolved, emotions become high, and people look for somebody who could guide them out of disorder.

In order to understand the trickster mode of operation, we need to review in some detail, what happens in uncertain and anguishing periods of transition. As the taken-for-granted order of things has become suspended, the form of conduct that were previously followed could no longer offer guidance. There is an intense search for new solutions with the mind being particularly excited. However, this coincides with emotional involvement, making the work of thinking difficult. In great distress, individuals look for each other in search of a solution or model to follow and, thus, can easily be induced to follow a course of action that otherwise they would never take, characteristic of crowd behavior, especially in panic, analyzed by Gustave le Bon, a contemporary of Nietzsche and a major source of the thinking of Durkheim, Tarde, Pareto, and Freud — and also, through Sorel, of Mussolini, Hitler, and Lenin. Thus, liminal situations jointly incite *both* reasoning *and* emotions.

Under such conditions imitative processes can easily spiral out of control, characteristic of violent mob action, even scapegoating, analyzed so well by René Girard or Gabriel Tarde. However, the situation is different if there are some people within the community who manage to use their sense and offer a solution. These are, in a Weberian terminology, the genuinely charismatic persons, who rise up to the opportunity and lead the community out of the crisis. The problem is that the same situations also favor tricksters, whose mind remains clear, as they are not emotionally involved in the community and do not have an interest in finding a solution. Quite on the contrary: As a trickster can only gain attention in a crisis, its only interest is in perpetuating situations of crisis. It can capture attention with slogans that *seem* to offer a way out — people in a state of distress are not terribly good in making distinctions, their sense of judgment being undermined — but that instead only spirals further the very forces that generated the crisis.

There can be two basic outcomes of such a situation, which can also be combined. If a temporary situation of crisis is perpetuated, we are faced with a paradoxical condition of permanent liminality[10] that is based on depersonalization and further promotes the same transformation from a person into a nonentity (Weber's "nullity"). The second main outcome is schismogenesis,[11] which means that a temporary breech or fracture in the social fabric, instead of being healed, is rather extended and aggravated until it becomes a permanent condition. The trickster logic here implies that instead of finding a way to close the gap and to resolve the conflict, the diverging positions are rather getting more and more distant from each other, until the previous unity is replaced by two sets of strongly different identities. Central for Bateson's concept is the modeling of the process by which the previous positions of identity are replaced by the two new identities, based both on the redefinition of the "self" and of the "other" and the progressive taking into account in the definition of the self how the other "labeled" this self.

The unfolding of schismatic processes is not a once-for-all event but rather, following the logic of "Bateson's Rule," one fracture can lead to another. Schisms can multiply with a new identity splitting into further halves. The European Reformation of the 16th century offers a perfect example, with fragmenting only stopped by all partners recognizing the others so as *not* to allow further destructive splitting, culminating in the establishment of the official churches. A similar example is offered by the socialist movements of the past centuries.

THE MINORITY PERSON

Without romantically overvaluing the challenges inherent in a minority existence, the anthropological concepts presented above offer a suitable framework for interpreting the particular position of members of ethnic or religious minorities.

According to Weber, the dynamic relations between ethnic groups can be described as a set of attractions and repulsions, while the groups themselves possess moral customs that can build communities.[12] Some authors place the emphasis on the boundaries between ethnic groups,[13] while others interpret ethnicity as a framework to perceive social differences.[14] There is consensus that the interpretation of national minorities must be situated with the relationship between the *nationalizing state* and the *kin-state*.[15] In this context, ethnicity or ethnic identity emerges through the interaction that is taking place between groups: Ethnicity "exists *between* and not *within* groups [emphasis in original]."[16]

The presence of minorities, or citizens who share a different culture or language, presents both an opportunity and a threat for the majority that usually possesses political hegemony. The assessment of minorities usually depends on the ruling political perspective: If a modern nation-state wants to demonstrate its own pluralism, it uses all political and legal means to demonstrate the existence and thriving of minority groups — especially outside its own borders—in order to receive recognition from other nation-states or supranational organization. Here, however, immediately a trickster aspect appears, through an internal contradiction, as a nation-state necessarily means national homogenization and, thus, strives for homogeneity. Thus, minorities regard the occasional tolerance of the local nation-state, just as the special favors offered by the distant kin-state, with due skepticism.

The moments and consequences of the collapses of empires are thus always different in the memory and interpretation of the "winners" and the "losers." The "winners," the majorities, found a home, while the minorities became losers, drifting into endless homelessness and entertaining new expectations while forced into an imposed political entity. Yet, at the same time, those with a shared culture and experiences generate close communities where the hope that the obstacles deployed against the free use of the proper language and culture would once be lifted. The daily life of a minority person is sometimes only latently, sometimes manifestly, penetrated by the dominant concern of preventing those actions of the majority that are supposedly oriented towards eliminating the very survival of the minorities.

The persons inside such (forced) communities, however, apart from the evident losses and deprivation, also received a chance[17]: As one's very existence became defined in contrast to the majority, often conceived as an enemy, this gave the opportunity of living, inside the modern world, as member of a particularly closely knit and personalized community, reversing — at this concrete time and place — the dominant modern tendency of depersonalization. Thus, living as a member of a concrete community offers the chance of intimate inwardliness (*bensőségesség*; a term quite different from individualizing but also depersonalizing privacy and intimacy), recovering a genuine dialogue all but lost in modernity. The dialogue of minority persons thus is not conducted between atomized and universal individuals, rather between persons who belong to the same ethnocultural community. The permanentization of such a dialogue might lead to a kind of inbreeding but can be an instrument for offering a transition from homelessness to a home. The realization of the hope of independence might shift a minority person out of this personalized world; thus, after the collapse of the Habsburg Monarchy or the Soviet Union several previous minorities suddenly became majorities, thus founding a home, and as the "new victors" started to act in every manner according to the logic of the majority nation-state, even in confrontation with their own new minorities.

A minority person can choose between several life strategies: One can take upon oneself a mediating role between the various linguistic, ethnic, and political entities (different minorities or the various, neighboring nation-states), but one can also follow the policy of separation or even of some or other versions of ethnic resistance. Whatever strategy is chosen, the actions will be pervaded by some kind of hope and the public demonstration of this hope. In the first strategy, it is the idea-ideal of "eternal peace" or "tolerance" that transpires, while, in the second, a belief in autonomy of one kind or another (individual, institutional-cultural, or territorial). A minority person always lives in some kind of belief, hope, teleology, or in an eternal in-between state and, thus, can easily be deluded, especially if someone evokes danger, crying wolf. And danger or threat is never far from the horizon of minority existence; a minority person, if only to heal or at least to sooth a trauma, needs to believe in a better world to come. So, a minority person must build on this paradoxical, as if structural *metaxy*-existence,[18] on the bridging between present and future, good and evil, no-longer-majority and yet-still-minority, or only-minority and not-majority.

The minority elite works on these same bridging, often accepting and even feeding those ideologies and hopes that could tilt the minority into a fulfilled future. This requires a certain imitation, the imitation of the elite behavior by minority members, which also offers an opportunity for various internal and external tricksters to appear. By internal tricksters, we mean those individuals or ideas that, already before adherence to a minority community, were connected in one way or another to the "saving" of the minorities; whereas, external tricksters are those potential saviors or ideas that attempt to "save" the presumed minority community subsequently and from the outside. Here, it is important, at least in a Central-Eastern European context, to emphasize the role of the "home country" (where the ethnic minority of one country constitutes the majority in another), where political actors, and not always for the right kind of reasons, come to emphasize the solution or "arrangement" of the minority problem or the "saving" of the minority persons considered as "authentic."

The relationship between kin-state politicians and the minority community can be characterized by mutual, calculative, mistrustful incomprehension, thus involving irresolvable contradictions. In order to understand the inherent trickster aspect of this relationship, we first need to realize that, no matter how such communities are unified, they still contain their own inner differentiation. While, due to their common goals, minority persons behave in a quite similar manner, they have certain segments, whether in a regional or social sense, which contain sociocultural essences that resonate better with the kin-state actors — or at least make them pretend so.[19] Such an entangled relationship can be considered as a joint trick of the kin-state majority (or at least its political representatives) and the minority, against genuine pluralism, where some kind of mutual imitation is staged, in order to reach some kind of proclaimed authenticity.

Minority persons often act as if they were a majority, only demonstrating their minority being by this very feature. They identify themselves with a minority existence as if they were not at all like that: They politicize and act as if they were the majority, even bracketing their minority identity. This even applies to the more "authentic" minority persons, who — meeting somebody from the kin-state majority — can easily gain inspiration for forgetting their own minority identity. But how is this possible? It is based on two premises: On the one hand, the minority person is capable of using an ambivalent language,[20] through which it can discursively appropriate the complex and manifold minority–majority relationship. On the other hand, a majority member of the kin-state by visiting the minority communities might leave for a time his own social existence, entering the personal world of minority communities that are perceived as authentic. This is an indication of the bipolarity of the modern world between individual and person.

In the minority community, the member of the kin-state is not "indigenous" but rather participates in an alien world where one knows the language and — to some extent — the culture. The perceived closeness of the minority people and the authenticity experienced actually strengthens a "trickster" identity in the kin-state person, who comes to believe that one can actually "save" the minorities through one's own means. The question is to what extent this benefits the minorities. Perhaps, by making them forget even more their minority existence, as the (external) kin-state trickster elevates them to such heights where only majority persons can accede. This thus offers one a certain experience of authenticity, which, however, is very different from the need for authenticity demanded by kin-state persons. Still, on the part of both sides such acts become means for a further depersonalization or an escape from one's own inner void. It remains to be seen to what extent they merely fall into each other's traps, and whether they will be capable of a genuine dialogue, of a similar living and interpreting of space and time. A minority person is not always dreaming about somebody saving him, thus the kin-state politician can easily lose one's charismatic aura, revealing his role as the savior of minorities as a mere mask. Thus, one can well imagine the relationship between minority and kin-state persons as one of a mutual and watchful glaring at each other from a distance.

The minority person himself, and any encounter with him have a liminal character. The emergence of such a mode of existence is always due to some kind of social schism, often of a multiple kind, and one's further, traumatic life is conduced on the borders between various worlds, often even encompassing the role of the victim or the scapegoat. In encounters between various minorities and majorities, however, not only the majority persons can redefine their own positions, even themselves, but even the minority persons. Such continuous, dynamic transitions can produce new and new minority identities, which the "majority" might try again and again to understand or — due to its desire to transcend itself by such identification —incorporate and thus abolish.

THE MEANINGS OF MINORITY EXISTENCE

It might seem strange that all the chapters in this volume deal with marginal areas of Europe; in fact, mostly of extremely marginal areas. While we cannot claim comprehensiveness, not even full representativity, this is by no means accidental. The problem of minority existence *is* indeed something characteristic of the margins of Europe, and not of its — broad — center.

Even further, practically all the areas discussed in the chapters fell outside the area of the former Roman Empire. This is all the more strange as the question of empires, their rise and collapse, was extensively discussed in the chapters, including — quite prominently — the Byzantine world or the Eastern Roman Empire. Yet, here again, the western core is out of the scope.

The reason concerns the specific affinities between empire-building, nation-state-building, and homogenization. Empire-building is driven by an insatiable drive for conquest, the very insatiability fueled by an inner void and, thus, the loss of meaning. The more the empire is extended, the more it conquers and formally incorporates areas that it cannot properly integrate culturally. Thus, the inevitable collapse of any empire leaves behind itself, after the devastation, a void — the same void, as if multiplied, or involuted, to which its very existence was due.

The void was filled, after the collapse of the Western Roman Empire, by the emerging nations, where life was maintained and given meaning by the Christian Church. After the schism of the Reformation, this eventually led, after the treaty of Westphalia, to the emerging absolutist states. The revolutions transformed the absolutist states into unified nation-states, but — as Tocqueville realized so well — by no means altered the drive towards centralization and uniformity. Such developments, far from representing "progress" in an absolute and universal sense, rather implied the formation of an increasingly homogenized and standardized world in which the insatiable centralization of states and markets (meaning the *stock* markets, one of the most centralized institutions ever invented on the planet) could progress jointly with a similarly streamlined individualization.

For a series of reasons, this "progress" was blocked in the eastern part of Europe and its surroundings — mostly for the worse but, in some ways, perhaps also for the better. While within its core areas, Islam produced, with its own means, a similar kind of homogenization in the broad lands between the margins of western Christianity and Islam, areas in close contact with (if not outright under) the Eastern Roman Empire and thus, following Eastern Orthodoxy, ethnic and religious diversity survived. This happened because the successive eastern empires (Byzantine, Ottoman, Austrian — literally "Eastern" — and Russian/Soviet) failed in both counts where the West succeeded, in the full ambivalence of the term "success." In the West, after the relatively early collapse of the Roman Empire, a Christian civilizing process emerged, resulting in meaningful and coherent communities, guided by the three major estates (Church, aristocracy, cities). These entities, after the collapse of the unity of western Christianity, "succeeded" to build, both using and abusing the previous civilizing process, ever more homogenized and centralized states, becoming ready to accommodate the new idols of mass democracy and mass markets, while external, overseas colonial expansion offered ways to increase resources and exteriorize conflicts. In the East, continental imperial expansion remained the objective, which, however, repeatedly failed to produce integration. The result was the coexistence of weakly integrated centers and a surviving manifoldness of local communities, many of which contained strange mixtures of local, indigenous communities: survivals of failed imperial centralization and homogenization, and migrants brought in to fill the void left by withdrawing or collapsing empires.

POLITICAL ANTHROPOLOGY: ETHNIC & RELIGIOUS MINORITIES

This is the context into which the various stages of western-driven "modernization" projects can be inserted. These projects are, since centuries and with very little learning from previous mistakes, a curious combination of pure extensions of the colonial mentality — exploit the region, just as the colonies, in the interests of the mother country; a taken for granted and self-assertive "civilizing mission," very different from the original goal of Christianization; and a desperate effort to clean up and contain the mess, once the instability of the region was threatening the core countries themselves. This implied, first, a conscious effort to maintain the empires (Austrian, Russian, even Soviet) in order to contain the indiscriminate "savages" of the "East"; then, after the collapse of these empires, an — often even genuine and well-meant — effort to extend there the benefits of modern civilization without being aware, in the minimal degree, of the considerable human price involved in such a homogenizing and liquefying "civilizing" effort; thus, as an inevitable result, the increasingly mechanized responses offered by the irritated center that failed to perceive the limits of its own dogmatic Kantian rationality, thus only perpetuating and fixing fault lines in the margins. Given the utmost lack of knowledge, interest, and care by the center in local affairs, and an arrogant belief in the superiority of its own abstract, "rational," constructed institutions, such efforts — just as in the former overseas colonies — created potentially explosive situations, held together by the threat of force, while the enforced requirement of identification alongside rigid and absolutized lines time and again only tore up wounds, unmaking healing processes that at the local level emerged due to the natural effects of the passing time. Institution-tinkering does not offer any solution, only tries to freeze conflicts, without healing root causes, and often at a similarly high price that the fooled migrants of our days had to pay for their "agents." Genuine personalities and communities are not mere constructs, so "constructing" institutions only freezes, temporarily, the situation, instead of offering a stable, long-run solution; thus, in the remarkable expression of Jesenko Tešan, a perpetual peace treaty, modeled on the work of Kant, only generates a permanent, frozen war.

Such western, enlightened, and absolutizing dogmatism was complemented in the East by the particular virulence of a trickster logic that is bound to emerge and rise to dominance in marginal border zones where and when transitioriality becomes increasingly permanent. The achievements of the West, which were partly genuine but partly only outcomes of a merely quantitative growth of power, generated by social and human homogenization, a precondition of technological growth, as Heidegger, Mumford, or Borkenau perceived so well, had to be transmitted to the East; and such mediation, communication, commerce, transport, and traffic is a prime area for the trickster, captured particularly well in the figure of Hermes. Such tricksters might thrive in nation-building, being more "patriotic" than any locals, or might, on the contrary, bemoan the hopeless backwardness of their countrymen, forcing them to follow the tide of "progress," as they only know it better. Most importantly, they might shift with stunning speed from one position to the other.

Such marginal areas, which are also liminal due to their mediating or in-between character (between East and West, North and South, Catholicism and Protestantism, Roman and Orthodox Christianity, Christianity and Islam, etc.), are particularly prone for falling into a mimetic escalation, which provides a further breeding ground for trickster figures to emerge and thrive, preventing any return to normality, given that confusion is the condition of possibility for tricksters to gain and maintain power.

In the case of ethnic and religious minorities, the possibility of such trickster logics becoming dominant are even more evident, as the chains of mediation are even longer, and, thus, their possible abuses greater. This is all the more so as such mediation often progresses through images, and it is very easy to appropriate and abuse images. In such trickster exchanges between the "progressive" center (or quasi-center, itself a mime of the "really" progressive western core) and the "backward" region, two sets of images are particularly attractive and are used in most case studies, including Ireland, where the East–West direction is of course inverted. On the one hand, irresistible images of wealth, health, progress, and development are transmitted to the backward regions, telling the tale of what expects those who fall in the line of progress, giving up every remaining segment of their "non-modern" "identity." Such images can of course be appropriated and retransmitted by local, "alternative," modernizing centers, who try to claim that such progress can only be provided through their own, "communist," "nationalist," or "national-socialist" ways. On the other, images of the "backward" area as hapless, suffering victims are spread in the center, catering for pity, while the same images are also deployed in the marginal areas, mobilizing for a politics of suffering, which can in its due course contaminate the center as well, reducing politics from an effort to promote public good to an impossible effort of eliminating all suffering from the world, alongside the now most influential, Habermas-Rawlsian political philosophy. It is in this sense that the situation of minorities can be taken as a mirror of the situation of the entire marginal region — and not only.

Thus, at one level, the situation of such minorities, reflecting the situation of the entire region, is utterly hopeless. They are chasing a dream that is proved to be a mirage in the center itself, the mirage of a happy and wealthy nation-state — just as those migrants who, in their own desperate situation, are only too happy to believe those tricksters who evoke for them the dream of living in the West, cheating them out of the small but real possessions they actually had. Yet, on the other hand, their very marginality might indeed turn into a value on its own. The chapters hint at two possibilities in this regard. First, marginality, for better or worse, can turn into liminality, and this might offer unprecedented connections and insights—as liminal conditions and situations are unpredictable—and may touch even upon the highest degree of liminality, in between the divine and the human — though the possibility of trickster interference is also the highest here. Second, on such margins, in certain ways always and necessarily outside the scope of the centers, modes of living different from the mechanized homogenization of the center can also persist. Combined with the previous point, this, after all, offers nonnegligible hope.

CONCLUDING COMMENTS

Permanent liminality, combined with schismogenic processes, is a paradoxical state that, however, cannot be escaped from those inside, recalling the terminology of "iron cage" or "entrapment" with which Max Weber characterized the modern condition. Reasoning, in particular, is unable to offer any guidance, as it is caught in the web spun from the outside by uprooted, eternally homeless trickster "rationality," which is unsuited to understand political reality that assumes participation and embeddedness in concrete communities. Yet, the rising dominance of trickster reasoning is helped by modern science, which is entrapped in its own — vicious — exterior circularity, based on the void that has evident parallels with the void of the "free and open" public sphere, jointly generating a condition of unreality where, instead of charismatic leaders, trickster politicians are emerging and increasingly dominate, through the "public sphere," the space of modern politics emptied of real presence.

FUNDING

Work on this special issue received support from the University College Cork Strategic Research Fund and the Centre for Social Sciences, Hungarian Academy of Sciences.

NOTES

1. For further details, see Agnes Horvath and Arpad Szakolczai, "Political Anthropology," in Stephen Turner and William Outhwaite, eds., *Sage Handbook of Political Sociology* (London: Sage, forthcoming); Ted C. Lewellen, *Political Anthropology: An Introduction*, 3rd ed. (Westport, CT: Praeger, 2003); Bjørn Thomassen, "What Kind of Political Anthropology?," *International Political Anthropology* 1(2): 263–74 (2008); and Bjørn Thomassen and Harald Wydra, eds., *Handbook of Political Anthropology* (Cheltenham: Edward Elgar, forthcoming). Concerning its application to nationalism and ethnic conflicts, see Thomas Hylland Eriksen, *Ethnicity and Nationalism: Anthropological Perspectives* (London: Pluto Press, 1993).

2. For details, see Arpad Szakolczai, "Empires: Rise, Decline and Fall," in Bryan S. Turner, ed., *Wiley-Blackwell Encyclopaedia of Social Theory* (Blackwell: Oxford, forthcoming).

3. Wilhelm Hennis, *Max Weber: Essays in Reconstruction* (London: Allen & Unwin, 1988).

4. Max Weber, "Politics as a Vocation," in H. H. Gerth and C. Wright Mills, *From Max Weber: Essays in Sociology* (London: Routledge, 1948), 128.

5. Max Weber, *The Protestant Ethic and the Spirit of Capitalism* (London: Allen & Unwin, 1976), 182.

6. Max Weber, *General Economic History* (New Brunswick, NJ: Transaction Books, 1981), 369.

7. For further details, see the various issues of the peer-reviewed journal *International Political Anthropology*, http://www.politicalanthropology.org.

8. Concerning liminality, see, in particular, Agnes Horvath, Bjørn Thomassen, and Harald Wydra, eds., *Breaking Boundaries: Varieties of Liminality* (New York: Berghahn Books, 2015); Bjørn Thomassen, *Liminality, Change and Transition: Living through the In-Between* (Farnham Surrey: Ashgate, 2014). The classic works are Arnold van Gennep, *The Rites of Passage* (Chicago: University of Chicago Press, 1960; originally published 1909); and Victor Turner, *The Ritual Process: Structure and Anti-Structure* (New York: De Gruyter, 1969).

9. See Paul Radin, *The Trickster: A Study in American Mythology* (New York: Schocken, 1972); Agnes Horvath, "Mythology and the Trickster: Interpreting Communism," in Alexander Wöll and Harald Wydra, eds., *Democracy and Myth in Russia and Eastern Europe* (London: Routledge, 2008); *Modernism and Charisma* (Basingstoke: Palgrave, 2013); Agnes Horvath and Bjørn Thomassen, "Mimetic Errors in Liminal Schismogenesis: On the Political Anthropology of the Trickster," *International Political Anthropology* 1(1): 3–24 (2008).

10. See Arpad Szakolczai, *Reflexive Historical Sociology* (London: Routledge, 2000), 215–26; and Arpad Szakolczai, *Permanent Liminality and Modernity* (London: Routledge, 2017).

11. See Gregory Bateson, *Naven* (Stanford: Stanford University Press, 1958); Gregory Bateson, *Steps to an Ecology of Mind* (New York: Ballantine, 1972); and Horvath and Thomassen, "Mimetic Errors in Liminal Schismogenesis," 3–24.

12. Max Weber, *Economy and Society* (Berkeley: University of California Press, 1978), 387–93.

13. Thomas Hylland Eriksen, *Ethnicity and Nationalism. Anthropological perspectives.* (London: Pluto, 2010), 43–69.

14. Rogers Brubaker, Margit Feischmidt, Jon Fox, and Liana Grancea, *Nationalist Politics and Everyday Ethnicity in a Transylvanian Town* (Princeton: Princeton University Press, 2006).

15. Rogers Brubaker, *Nationalism Reframed: Nationhood and the National Question in the New Europe* (Cambridge: Cambridge University Press, 1996).

16. See Thomas Hylland Eriksen, "Ethnic Identity, National Identity and Intergroup Conflict: The Significance of Personal Experiences," in Richard D. Ashmore, Lee Jussim, and David Wilder, eds., *Social Identity, Intergroup Conflict, and Conflict Reduction* (Oxford: Oxford University Press, 2001), 42–70, 46.

17. See Nándor Bárdi, *Tény és való: A budapesti kormányzatok és a határon túli magyarság kapcsolattörténete* (Pozsony: Kalligram, 2004), 29–30; and Nándor Bárdi, "Different Images of the Future of the Hungarian Communities in Neighbouring Countries, 1989–2012," *European Review* 21(4): 530–52 (2013).

18. See Eric Voegelin, *Anamnesis* (Notre Dame: University of Notre Dame Press, 1978).

19. In the Hungarian context, these are the *székely*-s (Szeklers) or even the *Csangos*.

20. See József D. Lőrincz, "Ambivalent Discourse in Eastern Europe," *Regio: A Review of Studies on Minorities, Politics, and Societies* 7(1): 148–71 (2004).

Trickster Logics in the Hungarian Dual-Citizenship Offer

ATTILA Z. PAPP

This article argues that the option of dual citizenship, available since 2010 for Hungarians living abroad, carries the possibility to create new types of national and civic identification patterns. This process can be considered as liminal, since it attempts to modify the nature of minority identity that was created by historic traumas and became institutionalized as social order, and because it attempts to open a new chapter in the relationship between Hungary and the Hungarian minority communities abroad. Although the patterns of the new (citizenship-influenced) minority identity are already somewhat visible, the full elaboration of this identity is yet to come. Therefore, the "managers" of the identity change might become tricksters.

INTRODUCTION

The Hungarian Parliament amended the Law on Citizenship in May 2010 and, starting from January 2011, allowed persons with Hungarian ancestry and language knowledge but without permanent residence in Hungary to naturalize in Hungary in a simplified procedure. This act resulted in more than 700,000 new Hungarian citizens, who in fact are dual citizens, as they kept their original citizenships.[1] The primary target group of the law are Hungarians living in the Carpathian Basin, but Hungarians living elsewhere (such as Western Europe, United States) also applied for Hungarian citizenship in great numbers. Among the neighboring countries, Slovakia made countermeasures and banned dual citizenship. New Hungarian citizens — despite their lack of Hungarian address — are eligible to participate at the Hungarian parliamentary elections.[2]

Dual citizenship implies a certain flexibility outside the aggregate of classic rights and responsibilities.[3] More citizenships can get hierarchically arranged and can affect the individual's contextual experiences of identity. This article presents some of the identity elements of minority Hungarians based on a qualitative empiric research[4] and draws up the changes that dual citizenship can bring to the minority identity.

The official argument for accepting the new law on dual citizenship was to help Hungarians over the borders. However, I think the creation, acquisition, and political benefit of dual citizenship are penetrated with trickster logic.[5] This will be explained in details at the end of the article; here, it suffices to say that all the circumstances are given for this logic to emerge. Members of the national minority live in a liminal condition, since their existence is the result of a historic and political schism of which they were mere victims. Minority status can be a permanent transition, which in Central Europe is associated with the intellectual hope that leaders should elaborate an ethical-based, authentic life conduct that will then be adopted by minority persons. This hope, however, evolved into the expectation of leaders who will come and show the way out of the problems. This hope, first of all, raises the responsibility of the elite and, second, raises the question: From where can these leaders emerge? From the minority society, from the kin-state, or from the nationalizing state? In the example of this article, dual citizenship was offered by the kin-state, but it is clear that "saviors" have come from the minority community and from the nationalizing state as well.[6] While the acquisition of this new Hungarian citizenship has a strong symbolic power, the application for citizenship is driven by rather pragmatic interests. Therefore, the universal flexibility and afforded playfulness of dual citizenship become apparent, and the questions arise: Was this the interest of the tricksters, and to what extent are the new citizens aware of the dangers of this playfulness?

In order to understand the emerging trickster logic of offering new citizenship for Hungarians living in countries other than Hungary, firstly, I try to describe some major element of the minority identity. After this, I will point out possible new identity patterns generated by dual citizenship, and finally I will argue why this dual citizenship is built on trickster logic.

MINORITY IDENTITIES: LEVELS OF CONNECTION AND RELATIONS

It is not easy to talk about minority identities in general, because that would assume an a priori given entity. In the approach of this article, it is admitted that the ethnic identity is a construction that can be understood through the practical application of certain categories. Ethnicity and identity are not taken for granted; they become actual in certain situations, and could be means of self-representation.[7] Although focus-group discussions are artificial situations, the discourses created in these situations reflect social practices that are significant for the respondents.

Having acknowledged these analytical insecurities, this article will use Brubaker's concept[8] as the starting point, assuming that, as the result of the new identities initiated by Hungarian dual citizenship, new Hungarian citizens will somehow relate to their country of residence (or the titular nation), to Hungary, and to their own minority community. This is a legitimate approach to understanding identity's link to citizenship, because dual citizens have to, both officially and/or informally, relate to their two citizenships. The identity options linked to the citizenships have to be mixed within the person's own world, as well as within his or her self-esteem process. This mixing inside can happen in an essentialist way, or through the cultural nation approach. In the latter case, the respondents interpret the acquisition of Hungarian citizenship as the direct result of their declaration of emotional belonging. Moreover, they are grateful to Hungary for offering the lofty opportunity of dual citizenship:

> I applied for it for mostly *emotional reasons*. I was among the first ones, at the beginning, when it was made available, we applied for it. It was important to me, I don't know, it strengthened a little bit my belonging there. (Interview No. 5, Ukraine, 11 Nov. 2013, emphasis added)

On the other hand, it should be noted that dual connection comes with a specific or mixed identification. This, however, does not create cognitive dissonance in the individual's mind, because this hybridity helps to reach an inner balance in everyday life. The dual connection, in this case, has a positive connotation. However, there can be instances where the balance on the discursive level is being created by mutual rejections or boundary-making.

> Well, I think that we here ... have to live if not with a *double identity*, but something like that, because we need to preserve, and normally we do *preserve our Hungarianness*, we need to live so that we remain Hungarians here. And it sounds a little weird, but for a certain extent we need to be *kind of Ukrainians*, just for the everyday life. (Interview No. 6, Ukraine, 11 Nov. 2013, emphases added)

The last quotation provides an illustration for the hierarchy of citizenships, which was mentioned earlier as a reference to Spiro. Even though the quote talks about identities, it also reflects statements about citizenship: One citizenship (and the identity linked to it) is important from an emotional perspective, in order to maintain the ethnic minority community, and the other citizenship is important for everyday lifestyle. However, from the group discussions, it became clear that the minority society is heterogeneous, referential, and often polarized. While one tends to imagine the minority community as homogenous, in reality, it is very diverse. This diversity can be detected through questions regarding where the individual belongs. In most of the cases, respondents answered this question with their local and regional ties and listed the broader "Hungarian" category only after these. However, there were some approaches of regional identity that can be interpreted from the perspective of identity politics. This perspective has a two-sided effect, since it affects both the interpretation of a historic condition and the opportunity of integration in the future. Identification categories such as "felvidéki" (from Upperland) or "délvidéki" (from Southerland)[9] do not only reveal understandings of history but also affect how one relates to Hungarian citizenship or to the Hungarian nation.

> *People use the terms depending on their aim.* Vojvodina is associated with the Serbian state, the Serb people, the entire term is linked to the post 1848 Serbian Vojvodina, and in general it is a political community within Serbia. Délvidék, on the other hand, would be a Hungarian region, that's the logic, but I don't think that it's so deliberate. (Interview No. 4, Serbia, 11 Nov. 2013, emphasis added)

In one of the discussions in Ukraine, respondents argued that the term "kárpátaljai" (Subcarpathian) Hungarian is an intellectual construction. In everyday life, Hungarians in Subcarpathia refer to themselves as Ukrainians to differentiate themselves from Hungarians of Hungary, even though they do not speak the Ukrainian language. (This is not surprising since a great part of Ukraine's population does not speak or use the language.) From the perspective of Hungary, one "sees" Subcarpathian Hungarians. However, a closer look reveals "Ukrainians" who do not speak Ukrainian and are native in Hungarian and Roma people as well.

> I think that those who call themselves *Subcarpathian Hungarians* want to set themselves apart from other Hungarians abroad, but not in a bad or pejorative way. And I think it happens rather *among intellectuals* because average people do not travel abroad, or to Hungary, where they are called Ukrainians, but they do not necessarily meet other Hungarians from abroad. (Interview No. 5, Ukraine, 11 Nov. 2013, emphases added)

The relativity of one's connections can also be traced to the definitions of home. While in the case of "homeland," there was a general consensus[10] (it is usually defined as the locality where the respondents were born and raised), the notion of "home" often becomes relative and approached from an identification perspective. Home is sometimes defined as one's homeland. However, it might be understood as a geographic location — a spiritual entity. On one hand, for those who define "home" as (pre-1920) Hungary or the Carpathian Basin, Hungarian citizenship is essentially a natural right.[11] On the other hand, for those who define home as their country of residence or their locality, Hungarian citizenship is a complimentary gift from the Hungarian nation (their mother country), which they can individually choose to accept or not to accept for pragmatic or emotional reasons. Those who consider the Carpathian Basin as their home can actually not decide whether they want Hungarian citizenship or not, while those who define a narrower territory (their country of residence) as their home do have the right to choose if they want Hungarian citizenship or not. Nonetheless, both "home discourses" very often brought up the concept of homelessness in the focus-group discussions and, from this perspective, Hungarian citizenship inevitably becomes the framework to resolve this insecurity. This, however, does not mean that the tension caused by the imperfect congruency of the concepts of "home" and "homeland" can be resolved:

> I'm from Vojvodina, I was born here, this is my homeland, Vojvodina is my home. *But now I start to feel* asserted, and *I am more secure now*. (Interview No. 4, Serbia, 28 Oct. 2013, emphases added)

> *We are Hungarians here, but Ukrainians in Hungary, and I would say that we might be homeless*. I feel like I'm a little homeless. I have a homeland, but an explicit home I do not have. (Interview No. 6, Ukraine, 11 Nov. 2013, emphasis added)

The respondents of the research were individuals who identified as Hungarians, and the discussions were held in Hungarian, so it is not surprising that they defined the knowledge of the Hungarian culture and language as the criteria of belonging to the (minority) Hungarian community. Beyond this dominant cultural nation approach, it was very interesting to hear the "borderline cases" — that is, the narratives of the liminality[12] of how they define Hungarianness. For example, we mentioned in the focus groups that, in the Hungarian western diaspora, there are many people who do not speak Hungarian but still identify as Hungarian.[13] The respondents disapproved of this phenomenon from the perspective of the cultural nation, but some narratives regarding the acquisition of Hungarian citizenship were also brought up. They admitted that there are people who get Hungarian citizenship without speaking the language, and this does not comply with the concept of ethnocultural nationhood, also known as ethnozenship. This phenomenon was presented in two different narratives. Some respondents said that it can be explained by the abuses of the preferential citizenship, and, therefore, they condemned it. Some even said that this practice questions solidarity; one of the respondents claimed that they did not apply for Hungarian citizenship because they do not want to identify with those ("liminoid") people.

On the other hand, in the other narrative this definitional insecurity was represented as positive, and the liminoid accessibility of Hungarian citizenship was interpreted as the extension of the borders of the Hungarian nation and, as such, it is not only acceptable but it also helps to tackle the insecurity inherent to the minority status.

> *Those who get the Hungarian citizenship, they will not have any problem with me anymore ... How shall I say this ... I interpret it as a positive, as a security thing from the Hungarian government, that whoever receives Hungarian citizenship, they will not point at me anymore, because they are Hungarians, too.* (Interview No. 4, Serbia, 28 Oct. 2013, emphases added)

A previous research (carried out before the adoption of the law that made dual citizenship available for Hungarians abroad) also revealed a minority ethnocentrism in Transylvania; respondents in that research described Hungarians in Hungary as strangers to them and amplified the differences between the two groups in a negative way, which generated a special minority ethnocentrism towards majority Hungarians.[14] In our current research, respondents were again asked how they perceive Hungarians in Hungary. The question is relevant in the context of citizenship because if it is supposed that Hungarian citizenship implies solidarity based on the shared culture, then there should be solidarity among the members of the nation as well. It seems, however, that there have not been any changes in the system of prejudices. Although some positive opinions were formulated about Hungarians in Hungary and about Hungarian institutions ("they are polite," "you can learn things from them," etc.), for the most part, the respondents emphasized the differences between themselves and Hungarians in Hungary. Thus, it can be claimed that the Hungarian–Hungarian boundary-making is constant, and it is especially strong when it comes to the question of belonging to the nation or using symbols. In other words, there is an insurmountable structural difference, an invisible barrier for Hungarians in Hungary; belonging to the Hungarian nation in their case is natural, and it does not imply any challenges. For Hungarians abroad, however, it is a matter of fate, and it is often emotionally charged. This structural condition affects the system of prejudices of Hungarians abroad; even though it is acknowledged that they do not form a real ethnic group, ethnicity for them serves as the major tool of boundary-making in relation to Hungarians in Hungary.

> *This thing* [Hungarian citizenship] *really means something only to us, for them we will still be a different cast or group, just like before,* so from this point of view it will not change. (Interview No. 4, Serbia, 28 Oct. 2013, emphasis added)

There is a theoretical and a practical side to this minority ethnocentrism. The theoretical side highlights the fact that previous research on citizenship did not address the minority Hungarian and majority Hungarian relations at all, although the concept of nation or membership in the Hungarian nation cannot be thought of as homogenous, as it would lead into the trap of "groupism."[15] The borders and the inner fragments of the nation have to be reconsidered and reinterpreted, since the nation itself is only a construction, not a primordial entity. The practical side concerns the possible effects of Hungarian dual citizenship that cannot be understood if the fractures of Hungarian–Hungarian relations are ignored. The special ethnocentrism of the Hungarian minorities might, however, result in a practical advantage as well. As Hungarians abroad will further become divided from Hungarians in Hungary by invisible barriers (besides their actual, legal secondary-citizen status), the divide might also prevent the diasporization of these communities. The constant re-creation of cultural habits and prejudices can thus extend the minority status of these communities.

PATTERNS OF NEW MINORITY IDENTITY GENERATED BY DUAL CITIZENSHIP

The "new" citizenship can slightly modify the identities attached to the "old" citizenship, and it entails new possibilities to interpret one's (minority) situation. This is even more probable if we consider the fact that, formerly, the category of "Hungarian" in a minority context did not include any citizenship identity[16]; on the contrary, being a Hungarian did not postulate Hungarian citizenship.

The conceptual opposites derived from minority identity and citizenship identity are necessary for two reasons. First, from a sociological or anthropological point of view, the identity attached to citizenship represents a greater challenge, since every kind of citizenship triggers identifications,[17] and both the minority and citizen situation implies specific identification possibilities. Second, although opposites polarize the differences of the two kinds of identities, yet we can claim — based on Koselleck's asymmetrical counterconcepts[18] or Weber's concept on ideal types[19] — that they are helpful in understanding the dynamics or the examined factors. The artificially contrasted identity patterns (see Table 1) do not imply that dual citizenship creates fundamentally new attitudes, rather — and this is what the empirical research showed, too — they refer to opposite, complementary habitual possibilities and individual strategies that evolve from the understanding of the new phenomenon.

TABLE 1 Elements of Identity Derived from Minority Status and Dual Citizenship

Elements of "Old" Minority Identity	Elements of "New" Dual-Citizenship Identity
"Jus soli"	"Jus sanguinis"
Perspective of staying	Possibility to emigrate
National framework	Transnational — relevant in "third" countries too
Hungarian Card	Passport
Imposed community	Freedom, electable
Insecurity	Security
Serious, "fate"	Potential for playfulness
Informal	Formal
Changes in time	Timeless
Everyday	Festive (symbolic)
"Being on the road" (homelessness)	"Arriving home"
(Important to) inward	(Important to) outward
"It is in constant training"	Eternal, permanent
Given, "it is there"	Deserved, "acquired," "received"
Contextual	Stable, "lasting paper"
Old	New
Multidimensional connections	One-dimensional, kin-state based homogenization

Minority identity is territory based, regulated by "jus soli," which is transformed by the Hungarian dual citizenship into "jus sanguinis" principle. The territory-based paradigm of "staying in the homeland" can easily be turned into migration potential after receiving a Hungarian passport; moreover, a Hungarian passport is even easier to access under materialistic considerations. Minority identity is interpreted in a national framework, in a loyalty system created by the existence of the majority state (the country of residence). On the other hand, dual citizenship is interpreted in a transnational framework, where, due to the migration opportunities, a Hungarian passport has relevance in third-party countries as well. This is why Hungarian citizenship has a greater weight than the formerly available Hungarian Card,[20] which, besides satisfying the (possible) emotional need of the person in a minority situation, had practical relevance only in the mother country, Hungary. The Hungarian passport, on the other hand, concentrates rationality and emotion, pragmatic and ethnic-emotional considerations at the same time. Furthermore, it sets free the dual citizens from the shame associated with the "old" citizenship and passport that was formerly experienced when traveling to Hungary or other countries.[21]

Minority identity was formed and consolidated in an imposed situation, which involved the imagination of inevitability, homelessness, and a range of microlevel experiences of abandonment. In contrast, the new Hungarian citizenship addressed the individual and, by doing so, it broke the feeling of abandonment and offered the hope of home. The individual responses to the call of the mother country bring a certain relief, and the seriousness of "fate" will be exchanged for the freedom of choice. The previous informal connections, as members of small communities, can now be turned into formal membership in the nation. This also means that Hungarian citizenship, as a formal, documented belonging, transcends time and offers the imagery of stability, contrary to the limited time interval attached to minority status. Minority identity has a starting point that reaches over the individual's life: Trianon (the place where the border changes after the First World War were concluded for Hungary, which thus became synonymous with the beginning of minority status for Hungarians abroad); whereas Hungarian citizenship represents a reparation of history, making time irrelevant. While Trianon is a metaphor for state borders switching above people's heads, the new citizenship is presumed to be an opportunity that transcends borders.

> I think, if we think about it, yes, now *we became part of a big community, or now we became part of it in a different way*. (Interview No. 3, Serbia, 29 Oct. 2013, emphasis added)

Although every member of the nation is eligible for the new citizenship, it still seems that people had to fight for it; and the fight was the minority status itself, the everyday life of minority Hungarians who were in constant training to maintain their identity. A date has become part of the faceless everyday life of Hungarians abroad: 5 December 2004, the date of the unsuccessful referendum on dual citizenship in Hungary.[22] This is a date that directs the attention to Hungarian-Hungarian relations and does not have positive connotations; even the current availability of Hungarian citizenship cannot erase it. In spite of this lack of success, receiving Hungarian citizenship is a celebration, marked by symbolic signs of belonging.[23] Festivity started to structure the use of space and time of the person in minority status in a different way and initiated an individual, new, returned era. Even though it offers opportunities of extrovert nature (for example, traveling) on the pragmatic level, on the emotional level, it provides the possibility of intimate "arrival," "homecoming," as opposed to the state of inner homelessness experienced many times before.

> When my grandmother got her Hungarian ID in her hand, she burst out in tears. She was born in Hungarian times... she has the ID next to her bed, it is displayed in the cabinet. *And she... she glances at it in the morning and she is not sick anymore.* (Interview No. 6, Ukraine, 11 Nov. 2013, emphasis added)

Minority identity partly derives from the "old," territory-based citizenship: This connection is evaluated on the neutral and negative axis of stigmatization. In the neutral sense, someone of minority status accepts the rights and responsibilities attached to citizenship (taxation, rule of law); however, in their narrative, this citizenship (and identity) often takes on the character of absence and, therefore, is often interpreted in a negative way. In this context, old citizenship can be the root and result of homelessness (for example, in Slovakia), the hotbed of corruption (for example, in Ukraine), and the manifestation of vulnerability (for example, in Serbia). The new Hungarian citizenship means an emotional plus in this context; it becomes the metaphor of pureness surpassing old citizenship, of true and honest connection, of freedom, and of light playfulness with no consequences.

> Now I am part of the community of ten, or now nine million Hungarian citizens. *And when I'm in Hungary, and a policeman pulls me over, I will give him my Romanian ID so he fines the Romanian.* (Interview No. 7, Romania, 4 Nov. 2013, emphasis added)

At the same time, certain old mental patterns can be carried over to the new citizenship as well. For example, if in Ukraine, citizenship is associated with corruption, then it can also mean that Hungarian citizenship can be acquired with the same practice:

> They did not speak Hungarian, of course. *You can buy the papers to certify your Hungarian ancestry, and that's where we stand.* (Interview No. 5, Ukraine, 11 Nov. 2013, emphasis added)

The elements of minority identity — as it was elaborated above — are being built on each other; they are often insecure, plastic, and relative. Labels used in Hungarian politics and everyday life ("Hungarians abroad," "transborder Hungarians," "Transylvanian Hungarian," "Vojvodina Hungarian," "Subarpathian Hungarian," "Slovakian Hungarian," or even "Ukrainian," "Romanian," "Slovak," "Serb," etc.) are only partially compatible with the self-identification of those concerned. Also, it would be an exaggeration to claim that there is full coverage between these labels. The usage of these labels is contextual, defined by social layers, and certainly shows the inner fractures of Hungarian communities abroad. In contrast, the perspective of Hungarian citizenship is homogeneity, since minority persons tend to focus on kin-state, and, therefore, there is a risk of ignorance of one's own minority community; it turns people living in heterogeneity or multiplied connections into the — theoretically and formally equal — members of the Hungarian nation. This perspective lays on national minority identity patterns the idea of equality that derives from citizenship. As a result, it can be interpreted as an attempt to eliminate minority status; furthermore, it also implies the perspective of becoming part of the majority society — meanwhile, it is clear that the extinction of minority identity elements would mean the disappearance of the minority.

POLITICAL ANTHROPOLOGY: ETHNIC & RELIGIOUS MINORITIES

EMERGING TRICKSTER LOGICS IN THE HUNGARIAN DUAL-CITIZENSHIP OFFER

As this article argues, the new Hungarian dual citizenship might transform the identity of minority Hungarians. It generates new hopes, but at the same time it homogenizes, redefining not only space and present but time and future as well. These are characteristics of the trickster, because he simplifies reality, does not take into account inner subtleties and, most importantly, communicates spectacularly and smoothly, through which his leadership skills are emphasized. Hungarian dual citizenship is part of the post-2010 political rhetoric, the System of National Co-operation,[24] and thus it became a communication act as well. Dual citizenship is a political good that can be communicated easily and, through that, the idea became enhanced that whoever has good verbal communication skills is a good leader. This communication act can have stronger effects in places where local dialects are used. Hungarian politicians arguing for Hungarian citizenship often make references to the "Szekler men" or Szekler jokes,[25] which implies the linguistic stigmatization of the local people,[26] but at the same time serves to prove their authenticity. Furthermore, this communicational behavior represents a dive into authenticity, the mimesis of expert understanding of Hungarian communities abroad, as well as differentiation on a linguistic basis.

As I mentioned earlier (see Note 1), the majority of Hungarian citizenship applicants are registered in Romania, Serbia, and Ukraine. Paradoxically, the Slovakian case demonstrates perfectly that the offer of citizenship is not more than a mimesis. Dual citizenship is not allowed in this country; Hungarians in Slovakia can only receive Hungarian citizenship if they renounce their Slovak citizenship. On the one hand, the interviews revealed that Hungarians in Slovakia would not apply for Hungarian citizenship in great numbers even if it was allowed. On the other hand, the Slovak countermeasure is trying to block an important nation-building project of Hungary and, therefore, should have resulted in negative Hungarian attitudes towards and relations with Slovakia. However, this is not what is actually happening; Prime Minister Viktor Orban — based on the real or perceived interests of Hungary — is cooperating with the prime minster of Slovakia, Robert Fico (in the Visegrad 4 interest group within the EU, or in the handling of the migration crisis).

The altruistic offer of citizenship is supposedly just one element in the trickster logic that is built on the consideration of whether or not to apply the principles of nation-building along the interests of neighboring relations, foreign policy, domestic policy, or other kinds of policies. These interests are not arranged in rigid hierarchy; they are organized contextually.

Hungarian politicians anticipated that dual citizenship would create a new social order both in Hungary and abroad. The supposition is correct that the "gift" of dual citizenship should develop new responsibilities and loyalties for Hungarians abroad. According to Marcel Mauss, a new social order is created by giving gifts, and everybody has to adjust to the new order.[27] In Hungary, dual citizenship filled an inner demand for legitimacy on one hand and, on the other hand, meant a new tool for foundation of national unity. As is stated in the Constitution, Hungary "shall bear responsibility for the fate of Hungarians living beyond its borders,"[28] and, because of historical reasons, dual citizenship can be a patronizing compensation for Hungarians abroad.

Trickster logic does not care about inner fractures, or the diversity of minority identifications and relations. It considers minority identity a challenge, a problem to solve. Therefore, offering citizenship is a great example of the trickster logic: It homogenizes and standardizes people. It does not consider the possibility, however, that by doing so, the authenticity of minority status can disappear. Neither does it consider that the target group is people who live in the socioeconomic subsystems of a different country; thus, their homogenization is problematic. Therefore, the trickster's main interest is to maintain the liminal situation, because, based on that, he can manipulate people according to his own interests and strengthen his position of power. To sum up, trickster logic actually wants to tackle its own problem of legitimacy demand, and Hungarians abroad are considered instrumental for this goal.

This logic was evident during the 2 Oct. 2016 referendum. For months, xenophobic, antimigrant discourse was going on in Hungary,[29] but the 50% minimum turnout that was necessary for a valid referendum was uncertain. Politicians of minority Hungarian parties abroad — supposedly after some pressure from the Hungarian government — tried to convince dual citizens to participate at the referendum and to vote for the rejection of the migrant quota. The trickster logic can be observed on various levels: Hungarians abroad applied for Hungarian citizenship primarily for emotional reasons, but, in this case, they were asked to become political actors. Furthermore, as was expressed in the focus-group discussions, political participation is not important for them, because they do not want to interfere in the affairs of a country where they do not reside. The trickster logic apparent in these two positions originates in the structural setting of dual citizenship; therefore, it is valid in any political participation that is linked to it.

There was another twist to the referendum. The topic of the political agenda at the referendum was about the rejection of migrants and inherently brought about increased levels of xenophobia.[30] By this point in the article, it must be obvious that minority Hungarians are often stigmatized as strangers in Hungary, and they have a hard time facing this attitude. They have firsthand experience of xenophobia in Hungary, to the same extent as in their country of residence. The following question arises: How can these people participate in a political spectacle of which they did not want to be a part, especially when they cannot identify with the role assigned to them? Here, the inner fractures of the minority society are relevant again: Approximately 15–20% of dual citizens with voting rights voted in the referendum,[31] significantly lower than the (also relatively low) 41% turnout in Hungary. The expectation of the great- and medium-level tricksters about the mobilization of dual citizens did not come true.

This instance showed the nature of the political trickster in Hungary—the play to encourage citizens to participate at the referendum—came to an end without catharsis. However, the trickster keeps on working: He overwrites the law, refers to the numbers that are favorable for his agenda[32] and gains momentum to act again, because his goal is to maintain liminality. If liminality is maintained, he has better chances to initiate actions to "save the nation," and he can again include in the fight those persons living as minorities but who received the promise of gaining majority status by acquiring Hungarian citizenship. However, trickster logic can become part of the dual citizens' everyday practices as well; they can play with and contextually use their citizenships. The following question arises: Who will eventually favor this institutional flexibility: the minority community or the kin-state? It is a possible scenario that neither of them will, and eventually the two actors will act together in the long term without any catharsis.

CONCLUSIONS

Members of the national minority live in a liminal condition, since their existence is the result of a historic and political schism of which they were mere victims. Minority status can be a permanent transition, a kind of in-between situation, which in Central Europe is associated with an intellectual hope, to which leaders will come and will show the way out of the problems.

Originally, the trickster denotes a certain kind of ceremonial master who emerges in liminal situations in order to "solve the problem." In this interpretation, dual citizenship created a liminal situation; more precisely, it amplified the latent liminality inherent to minority status. Dual citizenship stretched out liminality and generated new expectations and hopes. This stretched-out liminality is important for the trickster because his logic gains momentum more easily in this situation: He only has to pretend that he is solving the problem. However, it actually cannot be solved, except by creating new social schismogenesis.

NOTES

1. By April 2015, 716,662 citizenship applications were registered, out of which 446,603 were submitted by Romanian, 135,898 Serb, and 114,263 Ukrainian citizens. Thus, it is clear that Hungarians living in those three countries represent the majority of the applicants.

2. In 2016, there were 274,627 people eligible to vote; see the official website of the Hungarian Election Office: www.valasztas.hu (accessed 3 Nov. 2016).

3. Aihwa Ong, *Flexible Citizenship: The Cultural Logics of Transnationality* (Durham, NC: Duke University Press, 1999); Jonathan Fox, "Unpacking Transnational Citizenship," *Annual Review of Political Science* 8: 171–201 (2005).

4. In the framework of the research, there were nine focus-group discussions in Romania, Serbia, Ukraine, and Slovakia. Members of Hungarian minority communities living in these countries took part in these discussions.

5. Agnes Horvath, *Modernism and Charisma* (London: Palgrave Macmillan, 2013); Agnes Horvath and Bjørn Thomassen, "Mimetic Errors in Liminal Schismogenesis," *International Political Anthropology* 1(1): 3–24 (2008); Bjørn Thomassen, *Liminality and the Modern. Living Through In-Between* (Farnham Surrey: Ashgate, 2014), 99–105; Szakolczai Arpad, "Liminality and Experience: Structuring Transitory Situations and Transformative Events," *International Political Anthropology* 2(1): 141–72 (2009).

6. Such was the hope in popular service in the interwar period, or in communism after WW2; Ágnes Horváth, "A Népszolgálat, a Szolgálat és a Nép között," in Nándor Bárdi, Tamás G. Filep, and József D. Lőrincz, eds., *Népszolgálat: A közösségi elkötelezettség alakváltozatai a magyar kisebbségek történetében* (Pozsony: Kalligram, 2015), 267–87.

7. About the inflation of identity concepts, see Peter Stachel, "Identitás: A kortárs társadalom- és kultúratudományok egy központi fogalmának genézise, inflálódása és problémái," *Regio* 4: 3–33 (2007). About the dynamics of ethnicity in and through the categories of minority and majority (Hungarian, Romanian) and their asymmetrical worlds, using the example of Cluj, see Rogers Brubaker, Margit Feischmidt, Jon Fox, and Liana Grancea, *Nationalist Politics and Everyday Ethnicity in a Transylvanian Town* (Princeton: Princeton University Press, 2006), 207–238.

8. Rogers Brubaker, *Nationalism Reframed: Nationhood and the National Question in the New Europe* (Cambridge: Cambridge University Press, 1996).

9. These labels were the names of today's Slovakia and Voivodina in the pre-1920 and interwar Hungary.

10. On the different interpretations of home and homeland, see Nándor Bárdi, *Otthon és haza: Tanulmányok a romániai magyar kisebbségek történetéről* (Csíkszereda: Pro Print, 2013), 9–18.

11. Cf. the idea of Arendt, where citizenship is "the right to rights"; Hannah Arendt, *The Origins of Totalitarianism* (New York: Meridian Books, 1951), 294.

12. Bjorn Thomassen, "The Uses and Meaning of Liminality," *International Political Anthropology* 2(1): 5–27 (2009).

13. For more detail, see Attila Z. Papp, "Ways of Interpretation of Hungarian-American Ethnic-Based Public Life and Identity," in Pál Hatos and Attila Novák, eds., *Between Minority and Majority: Hungarian and Jewish / Israeli Ethnical and Cultural Experiences in Recent Centuries* (Budapest: Balassi Intézet, 2013), 228–59.

14. Attila Z. Papp, "Az etnocentrizmus szerkezete kisebbségben — a fókuszcsoportos beszélgetések alapján," in Valér Veres and Attila Z. Papp, eds., *Szociológiai mintázatok: Erdélyi magyarok a Kárpát Panel vizsgálatai alapján* (Kolozsvár: Nemzeti Kisebbségkutató Intézet and Max Weber Társadalomkutatásért Alapítvány, 2012), 79–116.

15. Rogers Brubaker, *Ethnicity Without Groups* (Cambridge: Harvard University Press, 2006).

16. In contrast, the majority categories (Romanian, Serb) indicate both citizenship and ethnic belonging; Brubaker et al., *Nationalist Politics*, 231–37.

17. Peter J. Spiro, "Accepting (and Protecting) Dual Citizenship for Transborder Minorities," in Rainer Bauböck, ed., *Dual Citizenship for Transborder Minorities? How To Respond For The Hungarian-Slovak Tip-For-Tat?* (Badia Fiesolana: European University Institute, 2010), 7–8.

18. Reinhart Koselleck, *Futures Past: On the Semantics of Historical Time* (New York: Columbia University Press, 2004).

19. Max Weber, *Economy and Society* (Oakland: University of California Press, 1978).

20. The Hungarian Card is issued under the "Status Law" (2001), and it can be provided to ethnic Hungarians living abroad.

21. The shame associated with the Romanian passport was experienced by (ethnic) Romanians as well. Brubaker et al. claim in their book on Cluj that citizenship in practice often receives a stigma; see Brubaker et al., *Nationalist Politics*, 321–26.

22. The referendum question was: "Do you want the Parliament to pass an act allowing Hungarian citizenship with preferential naturalization to be granted to those, at their request, who claim to have

Hungarian nationality, do not live in Hungary and are not Hungarian citizens, and who prove their Hungarian nationality by means of a 'Hungarian identity card' issued pursuant to Article 19 of Act LXII/2001 or in another way to be determined by the law which is to be passed?" The referendum was not valid. See the Hungarian National Election Office webpage: http://valasztas.hu/en/ovi/197/197_0.html (accessed 18 Nov. 2016). It was clear during the campaign that the stake of the referendum was not the preferential naturalization itself but inner political struggles.

23. The concept of "signs of belonging" was introduced by Goffman. See Erving Goffman, *Relations in Public* (New York: Basic Books, 1971).

24. A document that intends to lay the foundation of the new social order after 2010 elections: Office of National Assembly: The Programme of National Cooperation (May 2010), http://www-archiv.parlament.hu/irom39/00047/00047_e.pdf. (accessed 19 Nov. 2016).

25. Szekler jokes are a special genre of Hungarian joke-lore. These jokes depict Szekler men as prudent, patient clever, and inventive. For other characteristics of Szeklers, see Andy Hockley: Who are the Székely? (2.) (February 2013) http://szekely.blogspot.hu/2013/02/who-are-szekely-2.html (accessed 5 Nov. 2016). One of the famous popular sayings—"Beer is not a drink, a woman is not a man, and a bear is not a toy"— has been publicly used by a prominent politician of the Hungarian ruling party, and it provoked a great dispute because of its inherent sexism.

26. The Szekler language is a Hungarian dialect with a special pronunciation.

27. Marcel Mauss, *The Gift* (London: Routledge, 2002).

28. See *The Fundamental Law of Hungary*, Article D (April 2011), http://www.kormany.hu/download/e/02/00000/The%20New%20Fundamental%20Law%20of%20Hungary.pdf. (accessed 18 Nov. 2016).

29. The referendum question was: "Do you want the European Union to be entitled to prescribe the mandatory settlement of non-Hungarian citizens in Hungary without the consent of the National Assembly?" See the Hungarian National Election Office webpage: National Referendum 2016 (October 2016), http://valasztas.hu/en/ref2016/index.html (accessed 2 Nov. 2016). The ruling party (Fidesz) campaigned for the No vote.

30. https://www.hrw.org/news/2016/09/13/hungarys-xenophobic-anti-migrant-campaign. Surveys carried out in Oct. 2016 reveal that, "Since it has been assessed, xenophobia in Hungary has never been as high as it is today." See Christian Keszthelyi, *Xenophobia Skyrocketing in Hungary, Surveys Reveal*, (November 2016), http://bbj.hu/budapest/xenophobia-skyrocketing-in-hungary-surveys-reveal_124920 (accessed 18 Nov. 2016), first paragraph.

31. There might be a trickster logic traceable here as well, since there are no official data available. Dual citizens could vote by mail, but they had to register beforehand. According to estimates, 38–40% of eligible voters registered, and (here we do have official data) 47% of those actually casted a vote. See the Hungarian National Election Office webpage: National Referendum 2016 (October 2016), http://valasztas.hu//en/ref2016/481/481_0_index.html. (accessed 2 Nov. 2016).

32. Despite the referendum not being valid because of low turnout, the prime minister has initiated the changing of the Constitution, based on the results of the referendum. See Katya Adler, *Hungary PM Claims EU Migrant Quota Referendum Victory* (October 2016), http://www.bbc.com/news/world-europe-37528325 (accessed 6 Nov. 2016).

"Liminal" Orthodoxies on the Margins of Empire: Twentieth-Century "Home-Grown" Religious Movements in the Republic of Moldova

JAMES KAPALÓ

In the 20th century, the Russian Orthodox Church, the Romanian Orthodox Church, and the Soviet atheist state each pursued missions that attempted to transform Moldovans into loyal and trustworthy subjects and to integrate them into new state structures. This article explores the "liminal" character of Moldovan identities forged on the Russian and Romanian borderlands through the prism of Moldova's "home-grown" religious movements. Grassroots movements led by charismatic and "trickster" religious figures "played" with dichotomies of the hidden and the revealed, innovation and tradition, and human and divine, succeeding in transforming the subject positions of whole segments of Moldovan peasant society. The resulting forms of "liminal" Orthodoxy have proved enduring, perpetually critiquing and transgressing canonical norms from the margins and subverting the discourses and narratives that seek to "harmonize" identities and to consolidate nation, state, and church in the Republic of Moldova.

For several hundred years, the historical Principality of Moldavia nestled precariously between empires and cultural spheres, between the Orthodox Christian Russian Empire to the east, the Islamic Ottoman Empire to the south, and the Catholic Hungarians and Habsburgs to the west. In 1812, Russia incorporated the eastern half, between the Prut and Dniester rivers, as the Russian Oblast of Moldavia and Bessarabia, with the western half of the territory of the historical principality some years later in 1859 becoming half of the new Romanian state. Today's Romania, Ukraine, and the Republic of Moldova each incorporate parts of historical Moldavia. This article deals with the religious aspects of history and identity in the 20th century in the eastern half of Moldavia, known today as the Republic of Moldova but historically referred to as Bessarabia.[1] Moldova represents a quintessential anthropological borderland as defined in the work of Rosaldo and taken up by many others working on the US-Mexico border.[2] The borderland is a place where two, or more, cultures or societies overlap, where hybrid populations have the potential to "subversively appropriate and creolize master codes, decentering, destabilizing, and carnivalizing dominant forms."[3] We can make sense of this through Szakolczai's assertion that borders, or the *limen*, fundamentally connect liminality, and liminal activities such as language, trade, and sexuality,[4] with marginality, being on the edge or the periphery,[5] thus creating centers of creative, or destructive, potential out of marginal border regions.

This article explores the "liminal" character of Moldovan religious identities that straddle state and symbolic boundaries through the prism of two of Moldova's "home-grown" religious movements of the 20th century, Inochentism and Archangelism. These religious movements emerged in the liminal/marginal time and space of the Moldovan border region at the decline and dissolution of the Russian Empire. Revolution, war, and more or less constant political and jurisdictional change were the backdrop to the emergence of charismatic leaders; men and women considered the physical embodiment or incarnation of divine, angelic, and saintly persons. The corporeal "living" manifestations of Christ, the Holy Spirit, Mary, the Archangel Michael, and the Prophet Elijah walking the Moldovan countryside represented "embodied" acts of resistance to the emerging totalitarian regimes and the competing religious institutions of the time that were seeking total control of the religious field and of spiritual life.

The Republic of Moldova is known for its territorial vulnerability, for the "frozen conflict" in Transnistria, a narrow border strip of a wider borderland that declared independence from Moldova in 1990, and the ethnic enclave of Gagauzia that was granted autonomy in 1994 following a brief armed standoff. Although both of these conflicts have religious dimensions,[6] this article will touch on these regions only tangentially. Instead, I focus here on processes of "schism" within Orthodoxy in Moldova as a whole and the production of "liminal" identities that defy resolution. The Republic of Moldova's religious culture straddles Russian Orthodoxy and Romanian Orthodoxy. Today, the majority of Orthodox believers belong to the Moldovan Orthodox Church, a self-governing church subordinated to the Russian Orthodox Patriarchate. A smaller number (difficult to estimate as census data do not ask respondents to identify to which Orthodox Church they belong) are members of the Romanian Orthodox Church's Metropolis of Bessarabia, which was "re-activated" by the Romanian Patriarch following Moldovan independence in 1992 and was fully recognized by the Moldovan state in 2006. The separation between these two religious communities is not a straightforward one based simply on national, linguistic, or ethnic affiliation; many Romanian-speaking Moldovans belong to the Russian Orthodox Church as do most of Moldova's ethnic minority communities such as the Gagauz and Bulgarians.

One of the complicating factors has been the controversy over the church calendar. Soon after the territory of Bessarabia passed from Russia to Greater Romania at the end of the First World War, the introduction of the Revised Julian Calendar by the Romanian Orthodox Church in 1924[7] provoked a religious crisis, especially in the western part of Moldavia (which had been part of the Romanian state since unification in 1862) and Bessarabia, both of which had strong monastic institutions with a traditionalist outlook. The introduction of the solar aspect of Revised Julian Calendar in the Romanian Orthodox Church[8] but not in the Russian Orthodox Church created a temporal "liminal" period between fixed feasts observed by the two churches, including Christmas, with the Romanian Church celebrating on the 25th of December (according to the western Gregorian calendar) and Russians on 7 January. Resistance to the new calendar resulted in violent confrontations between the Romanian Gendarmerie and the Stilists, or *Stilişti*, the term used to refer to those who continued to adhere to the old-style calendar, in the 1930s. For the Romanian Church and state, the calendar was a question of social, moral, and religious order of the new nation state[9] but for large portions of the Orthodox population it represented a cataclysmic break with tradition, with liturgical time itself, and marked a sign of the impending End of Days.

Both the Romanian and Russian Orthodox Churches, as well as, of course, the Soviet atheist state, pursued "civilizing" and "nationalizing" missions that attempted to transform Moldovans into loyal and trustworthy subjects and to integrate them into new state (and church) structures.[10] They were only partially successful in their aims due to Moldova's continual history of dislocations from states and temporary integrations into others. The permanent state of oscillation between different poles of gravity, Russia and Romania, in the 20th century created extended periods of weakened structures and ineffective, unfamiliar institutional systems, that equated to a state of perpetual crisis or a structureless "liminal" state, a magical "wonderland" where anything is possible,[11] especially in religious terms.

It is worth recounting here briefly the extremely complex history of shifting borders that followed the collapse of the Russian Empire as it stands testimony to the assertion that "anything can happen" with regard to borders in this region. The Russian province of Bessarabia established in 1812 was dismembered in 1856, losing three southern districts, only to be reformed in 1878. In 1918, it was ceded to Romania by the Great Powers. Following the loss of Bessarabia, the new Soviet regime "magically" created from parts of western Ukraine, where ethnic Moldavians constituted a sizeable minority, a new Moldavia, the *Moldovan Autonomous Soviet Socialist Republic* (MASSR), parts of which were later absorbed back into the new *Moldovan Soviet Socialist Republic* in 1940 when the old territory of Bessarabia was reoccupied by Soviet forces. This state of affairs lasted a little over one year until in July 1941, when Romania and the Axis powers invaded the Soviet Union and reoccupied the territory. Following the defeat of Romanian forces in 1944, the *Moldovan Soviet Socialist Republic* came back into being only without two southern counties of Bessarabia, Ismail and Cetatea Albă, and the northern district of Hotin, which were gifted to Ukraine. Following Moldovan independence in 1991, the territories of the *Moldovan Autonomous Soviet Socialist Republic* (MASSR) that had remained part of the *Moldovan Soviet Socialist Republic* after 1944 broke away to form the internationally unrecognized *Pridnestrovian Moldavian Republic*, or Transnistria as it is widely known.[12]

Amidst these territorial disputes and wars, a religious struggle was also under way. The Russian Orthodox Church between 1812 and 1918, intermittently but sometimes vigorously, pursued a policy of Russification of the local Moldavian Church. The Romanian Orthodox Church and state, likewise, attempted to Romanianize the Orthodox Church and the population of the province when it was in control. Mainstream church history of Moldova tends to frame the religious history of the territory solely in terms of the national struggle of the Romanian-speaking majority for control of the local church dominated by Russian hierarchs.[13]

Shifting state and religious boundaries such as these demand that actors, be they political, economic, or religious, engage in "boundary work." The religious actors discussed in this article frequently crossed borders between states, between religious communities, and between ethnic groups, displaying considerable ingenuity and creative spirit acting as mediators, translators, smugglers, and masters of disguise. If traditionalism can be considered a characteristic of identities in the region, particularly the largely agrarian territory of Moldova, this should be complemented with an appreciation of the ingenuity and mutable character of identities forged in border regions.[14]

This article briefly presents two cases that illustrate a complex picture of grassroots religious agency and fluid religious identities that emerged against this shifting backdrop. I introduce two charismatic religious leaders who in some sense displayed characteristics of the "trickster"[15] or had these characteristics projected onto them by their adversaries. These are figures that played with dichotomies of the hidden and the revealed, divine and human, and this world and the next world, and who succeeded in transforming the subject positions of significant segments of Moldovan peasant society. The resulting forms of what I term "liminal" Orthodoxy, groups that perpetually critique and transgress canonical norms from the margins, have proved enduring and continue to subvert the discourses and narratives that seek to harmonize identities and to consolidate nation, state, and church in the Republic of Moldova.

My research on religion in the Republic of Moldova is grounded in periods of ethnographic fieldwork amongst religious communities as well as archival research. Drawing on anthropology, folklore, and history, I explore vernacular knowledge, folk practices, and local memory as a counterpoint to national romantic narratives that tend to wash over religious, folk, and local cultural meanings. This article draws mainly on historical sources but my appreciation of the enduring significance of the characters and movements discussed here come from ethnographic observations of contemporary Moldovan society.

RELIGIOUS CHARISMA AND ROMANIAN VERNACULAR RELIGIOSITY

Before I give a biography of the two leaders, I present as examples of charismatic "trickster" figures, I will outline what I mean by "charisma" and "charismatic religion" in the context of ethnic Romanian folk religious culture out of which the two main protagonists emerged. Géza Vermes, taking Weber as his starting point, identifies and names a distinct and enduring current within Judaism that he referred to as "charismatic Judaism."[16] This form of Judaism relied on direct contact with the divine; "on the highest level, this stream was represented by revelation based prophetic Judaism" whereas, on the popular, grassroots level of folk or vernacular religion, it was "marked by charismatic manifestations of ecstasy and wonder."[17] This brand of Judaism gave to early Christianity many characteristic features: spirit-possessed prophetic ecstasy, healing, exorcism, wonder-working, bodily suffering to bring one closer to God, and embodied divinity are all characteristics that Christianity inherited from the prophetic tradition of Elijah, Elisha, Samuel, and others.[18]

Romanian popular religion is suffused with tales from and references to Jewish and Christian apocrypha that inform a rich folk cosmology with numerous supernatural and divine characters.[19] This tradition, revealed in both biblical and postbiblical literature, and expanded on in later Christian apocrypha and hagiography, found its way into the Romanian vernacular tradition through the manuscript tradition of the monasteries and later the publication of chapbooks. Popular books rich with apocryphal legends and the lives of saints were largely responsible for the appearance of theological themes in Romanian folklore as the borders between oral and written culture were particularly fluid.[20]

Of the wonder-working "Men of God" of charismatic Judaism, Elijah and Enoch stand out as they were carried up bodily into heaven without dying.

In this sense, they are peculiarly powerful figures with the ability to intervene in human affairs directly. Their unique status as "undying" prophets explains their association in the Romanian tradition with the passage in Revelation in which "two witnesses," will prophesy for 1,260 days before being killed by the Beast from the Abyss, and, after three days rise up on a cloud to Heaven (Revelation 11: 3–12). In Romanian apocryphal literature, Elijah and Enoch will herald in the end times by unveiling Satan's attempt to destroy the world and battling with him until they themselves are killed.[21] Badalanova Geller has highlighted the deep and enduring significance of the "Enoch Epos" on Slavonic Christian, and hence also Romanian, culture and thought.[22] In particular, she points to the association of living visionaries and saints in the Balkans with the name of Enoch that represents "a continuous and unbroken cognizance of the story of Enoch within the religious imagination of the region."[23] In the book of Genesis, Enoch is referred to as having "walked with God; then he was no more, because God took him away" (Genesis 5: 24). The fact that the Pseudoepigrahic Second Book of Enoch survives in more than 20 manuscript forms dating from the 14th to the 18th centuries is an indication of its popularity and a clue to understanding Enoch's widespread reception into the vernacular tradition. The most popular apocryphal narratives in the Romanian tradition close with the End of Days when "The Antichrist will come to enchant the world and kill Enoch, Elijah and Saint John and after three days they will be raised and the End of the World will begin. The powers of Heaven will move and all will be scattered."[24] The narrative of the End of Days is a powerful and integral aspect of Romanian religiosity and folk narrative and represents a period of transition when divine and human meet on earth.

Another particularly honored and almost ubiquitous figure in Romanian vernacular religious imaginary, and also closely associated with the End of Days, is the Archangel Michael. In some of the most widespread narratives, Michael is the companion and guide of the Mother of God and of Saint Paul in their respective journeys though hell,[25] he combats demons in the most well-known exorcism texts and healing charms,[26] and he sounds the trumpet at the End of Days; he is the prince of angels, a warrior, and taxiarch of the heavenly hosts who casts down Satan at the beginning of creation and as he does again at the End of Days.[27]

As already mentioned, the monasteries of Moldavia and Wallachia played an important role in transmitting and disseminating these narratives and ideas. The charismatic legacy of Judaism and late antiquity, which established a legitimate counterpoint to the clerical hierarchy, passed to the Holy Men and wonder-working *startsi* (elders) of Orthodox monasteries. The special relationship between monastic charisma and the Orthodox clergy has been described as a "paradoxical feature of Eastern Christianity."[28] Elders within the Russian Orthodox tradition, but especially the Moldavian tradition,[29] "straddle the boundary between the Church and the world" offering a perpetual counterpoint to the "bureaucratically rationalized institution."[30] They can be understood as mediators or "boundary-workers" between the world of local vernacular knowledge and learned culture. This particular relationship between the Holy Men of monasteries, who may or may not also be holders of positions of rank, and church bureaucratic power unfolded over several centuries in Orthodoxy. As Paert explains, "charismatic authority was a legitimate and sanctioned element of the Church's theology and practice" and, yet, they could also represent an "anarchic force."[31]

The idea of charisma in vernacular Romanian religiosity, therefore, is peopled by undying, ever-present supernatural characters from Jewish and Christian apocrypha who are destined to play central roles as embodied actors in the drama of the End of Days and that find their living reflection in the monks, exorcists, healers, and miracle workers of the contemporary monastic tradition.

INOCHENTIE OF BALTA

An Orthodox monk of Moldavian peasant origin, Ioan Levizor, who took the monastic name Inochentie, fits perfectly the model of a charismatic leader in the vernacular tradition outlined above. The earliest and most authoritative account of Inochentie's life and movement is by the Romanian Church historian Nicolai Popovschi published in 1926.[32] It contains a wealth of detail collected from contemporary written and oral accounts and tries to take an objective view. The other key source, largely overlooked by historians because it contains historically dubious events and numerous miracle stories, is the hagiography published by his followers, *Short Life and Deeds of Father Inochentie of Balta*.[33] Most other sources on Inochentism are antisect church publications or Soviet antireligious propaganda materials, which are very problematic as sources but nevertheless give us important insights regarding state and church attitudes, perceptions, and discourses.[34]

As already mentioned above, Bessarabian society in the first few decades of the 20th century passed through a period of unprecedented change. In terms of the religious landscape, the traditional dominance of Russian Orthodoxy was challenged by Tsar Nicholas's Edict of Religious Toleration of 1905. Introduced during the 1905 Revolution as a concession to appease his opponents, it opened the way for diverse groups such as Baptists and Adventists to gain legal recognition and at least nominal acceptability, adding significantly to religious diversity.[35] Rural Bessarabia in particular became especially diverse, having already received German Protestant settlers in the 19th century as well as waves of Old Believers, Molokans, and Skoptsy.[36]

In 1909, the religious revival sparked by Inochentie set the Bessarabian countryside alight. Born in northern Bessarabia in 1875, as a young man, he was inspired by visions of the Mother of God and having taken on the identity of a "Holy Fool" he wandered far and wide to the monasteries of Russia and Ukraine, including the famous Kievan Lavra of the Caves[37] where he was praised for his "angelic voice."[38] The religious revival was initially centered on the relics of a holy man called Feodosie Levitzki[39] creating a "Moldavian Lourdes" at the monastery in Balta (see Figure 1), a small provincial town close to Bessarabia in the Russian province of Kherson.[40] Soon, however, the pilgrims came to be focused on the apocalyptic preaching, exorcisms, and charismatic healing ministry of Inochentie himself. Much controversy surrounded the few short years of Inochentie's revival between 1909 and his death in 1917. The movement troubled the Russian Orthodox Church in the region to such an extent that the church removed Inochentie to the Russian Far North and the Tsarist authorities and church missionaries hounded his followers, soon labeled dangerous "sectarians."

Inochentie and his movement were considered dangerous for a number of reasons. Firstly, the movement took place in the sensitive border region amongst the Moldavian ethnic minority and so it was interpreted in political terms, as a reflection of Moldavian national aspirations, as well as religious terms.[41] Inochentie was a great orator in the local Moldavian language at a time when the local idiom was considered subversive by the state and Russian Church. He was, however, also well versed in Russian Church culture and was able to mediate local vernacular culture and elite church culture.

He was considered to have a "harmful influence" over the pilgrims visiting the monastery in Balta because he encouraged them to prepare for the End of Days and to forego marriage and sexual relations, overturning the sexual norms of peasant society.[42] He elevated women to positions of authority, endowing them with the honorific title of the Mother of God and granting them priestly apparel and status. The most characteristic belief associated with the movement was that the End of Days is very close indeed, a view believed to have been "borrowed from Baptists and Adventists."[43] In 1912 and 1913, followers of Inochentie calculated the time of the Final Judgement in a matter of weeks and months and when this failed to come to pass they considered that mankind was merely enjoying a reprieve thanks to the power of the prayers of Inochentie.[44] According to the testimony of Inochentie's followers, as human evil "becomes more terrible and the Devil entangles man in his nets, demons can enter people because of their sins and for this reason 'sin reigns in the world', and all of this 'can be perceived most clearly through the suffering of the sick.'"[45] The Inochentist conception of illness and possession has some unique characteristic elements that differ from the standard Orthodox view. Many of Inochentie's followers experienced an unusual condition of extreme spiritual distress.[46] This condition became so widespread that it warranted a special commission ordered by the Governor of Kherson province and the local

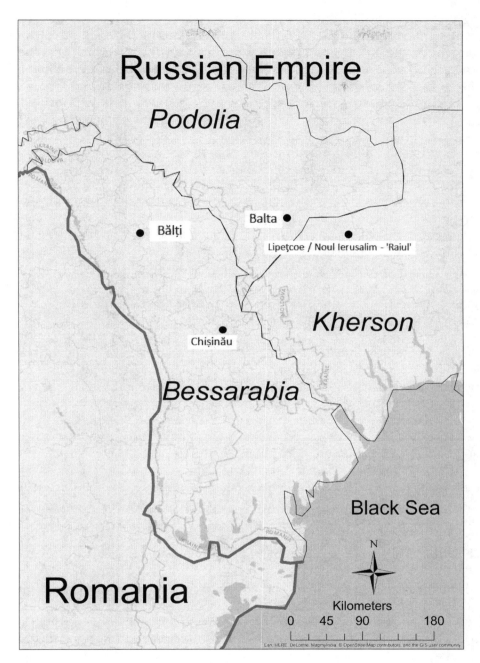

FIGURE 1 Map showing the place of origin of the Inochentist movement on the border between the Russian provinces of Podolia, Kherson, and Bessarabia. ©James Kapaló.

bishop, Dimitri, to investigate the religious "mass psychosis" taking place on their territory[47] according to which "the suffering of the 'possessed' were redeeming the world and preparing the way for the Kingdom of God."[48] The psychiatrist who undertook to examine those who were falling victim to this strange sickness, V. S. Yakovenko, published his finding in an article in the Russian journal of psychiatry, *Sovremennaya psikhiatriya*, in 1911.[49] The possession cult that emerges from these accounts bears one of the key hallmarks of I. M. Lewis's category of "peripheral possession."[50] Lewis regards certain forms of possession, those that are most often found amongst women and marginalized communities, and that are initially considered as an illness, as "thinly disguised protest movements," a kind of "clandestine ecstasy" that can be targeted against the dominant sex and power structures.[51]

More dangerous still than this apocalyptic fervor and associated possession cult was the identity of Inochentie himself. The apocalyptic expectation amongst Inochentie's followers intensified following his exile in 1912 and especially when he was interned in 1914 in the dreaded Solovetsky monastery, the notorious prison for Orthodox dissenters in the Russian Far North. Whereas initially followers of Inochentie spoke of him as a teacher and a holy man endowed with special gifts of healing and prophecy,[52] as the persecution of Inochentie and his followers intensified, Inochentie came to embody important characters in the scriptural and vernacular narratives of the End of Days, most notably the prophets Elijah and Enoch, the Spirit of Truth revealed in the Gospel of John and even the Holy Spirit. As already mentioned above in Romanian apocryphal literature, Elijah and Enoch will herald in the end times by unveiling Satan's attempt to destroy the world and battling with him until they are killed.

Popovschi asserted that "the harder Inochentie was pursued by the authorities the more his followers amplified their opinions on his personality. The ideas that Inochentie is the Holy Spirit first arose when he was sent to Murmansk."[53] The missionary manual penned to combat Inochentist ideas dedicates considerable attention to the problem of refuting the Inochentist claim that Inochentie is Elijah, Enoch, or John the Baptist walking the Earth again.[54]

As the pressure on Inochentie's followers mounted, Popovschi realized, they became less willing to openly discuss their beliefs.[55] And as church authorities progressively silenced Inochentists through their missionary campaigns, it was noticed that an iconographic tradition was emerging that represented visually the ideas that the church was condemning as heretical.

> Inochentists used icons with the image of Inochentie. So, in 1913, in some villages in Bessarabia, an "extraordinary envoy" of Inochentie, whose identity remains unknown, showed a photograph to the Moldovans in which are pictured God the Father, God the Son, and

FIGURE 2 Photograph of a mass-produced lithograph icon with Inochentie enthroned in heaven next to Christ with a dove at his breast symbolizing the Holy Spirit. This photograph was taken in the home of an Inochentist in the village of Lipețcoe, Ukraine. Photo ©James Kapaló, 2012.

in the place of the Holy Spirit, the monk Inochentie with an image of a dove at his breast.[56]

Such images (see Figure 2) became extremely widespread. Archimandrite Antim Nica, who was sent as a Romanian Orthodox missionary to the area around Balta during the Second World War, observed that "the image of Inochentie, in painted or photograph form, can be seen in Transnistria in many Moldovan families, placed between icons in the east corner of the house"[57] and adding later that "More clearly than in their pious writings, the beliefs of Inochentists are reflected in their iconography."[58]

When Inochentie was finally released from exile in the spring of 1917 following an appeal to the Holy Synod and aided by the events of the February Revolution, he returned home to the subterranean community, the

Garden of Paradise, his followers had dug in his absence near the village of Lipețcoe in Kherson province. Arriving in June of that year, according to his hagiography, he began once again to preach the Gospel of Christ, do great miracles and heal the sick.[59] He died soon after on 30 December 1917.[60] He was buried on New Year's Day 1918 in a small underground chapel prepared specially to receive his remains.

One final miraculous episode is recounted in a later, revised version of his *Life and Deeds*. On 2 October 1920, the Bolsheviks are said to have removed his remains from his tomb only to find his body, after almost three years, entirely intact and giving of an unearthly aroma of spices. When the commissar of the Bolshevik troops tried to rip the priestly cross from around Inochentie's throat he rose up from his coffin. The commissar fled in panic. Inochentie's body was taken that evening to the hospital in Ananiev and, when the doctor was about to cut into Inochentie with his scalpel, Inochentie began to breathe. In panic, the soldiers resealed the coffin and shut the room placing two men on guard. In the middle of the night, after being knocked out senseless by a loud noise, the soldiers came around to witness a cloud that rested above the hospital in which a great light shone. From the light came a pillar of fire from the ground up to the sky. The body of Inochentie rose out of the coffin and into the pillar of fire and up to Heaven in great glory,[61] a final indication of his identity as Enoch, Elijah, and the Holy Spirit embodied at the End of Days.

Inochentie's miracles, his life, and his suffering at the hands of the Tsarist authorities and the Bolsheviks were translated into a new divine narrative, full of biblical parallelism, for the changed political and social reality; divinity once again walking the earth and heralding in the End of Days. Out of the liminal crisis of revolution, "imitative processes suddenly multiplied."[62] In a process Bodin describes as the "typologization" of events, a "leveling" or "annihilation" of history was achieved in which "temporality itself is abolished. History merges with the eternal."[63]

ALEXANDRU CULEAC, THE ARCHANGEL MICHAEL

My second example, Alexandru Culeac, unlike Inochentie was a lay person with no connection to Orthodox Church institutions. In 1920, this 19-year-old boy from a remote corner of northern Bessarabia had a vision in which, after several trials and tribulations, he became endowed with the attributes of the Archangel Michael and took the title of "sfântului Duh arhangelul Mihail" — the Holy Spirit Archangel Michael.[64] Alexandru had four brothers: Ion, who became identified with John the Baptist, was referred to as "Tătunea Ion" or Father John; Grigore, who according to his own visions was Christ embodied on earth was referred to by his followers as "Dumnezeul viu pe pământ," the Living Lord on Earth; and Petru and Gheorghe, who were both modeled as saints and disciples of their brothers. The Culeacs went on to publish their visionary experiences and to immortalize themselves in numerous devotional images and photographs, spreading their message of repentance, divine immanence, and the End of Days throughout Bessarabia. The Culeac brothers, according to Soviet propaganda sources, convinced some of Inochentie's followers that had been driven underground to recognize them as his spiritual heirs and in this way inherited an already existing network of followers. The movement, most commonly referred to Archangelism, went on to constitute the most widespread and, from the perspective of the authorities, one of the most troubling illegal underground religious group in Moldova.

Alexandru's visionary career began in 1920 when he experienced a long and complex set of visions that he published in a booklet in 1924 under the title *A Vision That Appeared in the Year 1920*.[65] Grigore also had visions that he published under the title *The Visions of Grigore Culiac and his Sufferings for the Confession of the Second Coming of Jesus Christ*.[66] Alexandru, Ion and Grigore drew on the capital of their forerunners, Inochentie and Feodosie Livitsky, the holy man around whose relics Inochentie had built his flock. In their visionary texts, these two "prophets" herald in the future mission of the Culeacs. Alexandru's vision opens with a preamble that sets the stage for appearance of the Archangel Michael on earth:

> So it is said that the Archangel Michael will come to wage war with the Antichrist, and this he has done now and this is the witness of the two. As it was told 10 years ago by Father Inochentie and Saint Feodosie, so he is now doing in Bessarabia.

And to ensure there was no doubt about the identity of the Archangel Michael on earth, he adds:

> And these two great and powerful prophets, Father Inochentie and Saint Feodosie prophesied and said that there will come to Bessarabia young and old, great and small. They said there will come a youngster 17 years of age after him [Inochentie].[67]

Grigore too, after introducing his own visions as "heavenly [visions] of the second coming of Jesus Christ on earth in the flesh" refers to his forerunners, imploring Christians to have faith in Inochentie as Elijah and Feodosie as Enoch, the two great and powerful prophets who "prophesied and found the path to judgment."[68]

Taking on these divine identities, the brothers initiated parallel networks. According to later Soviet reports, they divided up the territory of Moldova between them.[69] The closing passage of Alexandru's vision of

1920 establishes three principal persons of the new movement, himself as Archangel Michael coterminous with the Holy Spirit, his brother Ion as John the Baptist and his wife as the Mother of God.[70] The evolution of the related but distinct groups the Culeacs founded is difficult to piece together but following the death of Ion in 1945, the Archangelists and Tătunists appear to have merged into one network under Alexandru and Ion's wife Ecaterina Stechi.[71]

By 1924, Alexandru had grasped the power of the image, and of photomontage and collage in particular, to convey his message of divine election and embodiment. In the image that appears in the frontispiece to his *Visionary text, O vedenie*, he is pictured as the Archangel Michael endowed with symbolic attributes, including a dove at his heart to indicate the composite identity of The Holy Spirit Archangel Michael. In 1946, the KGB reported the widespread presence of the "so-called Inochentist sect," which by this stage largely comprised Archangelists and Tătunists, "in almost every locality of Moldova."[72]

The Culeacs were masters of "border crossing." They crossed not only the literal territorial borders between Romanian Bessarabia and the Soviet Ukraine, proselytizing and trafficking between communities first established by Inochentie,[73] but more significantly the border between human and divine. One of the ways they did this, as with Inochentie before them, was through the use of evocative visual imagery in order to collapse sacred time with contemporary history and events.

CONCLUSION

Transitions "from one polity to another," according to Dumitru and Negura, characterize the last two hundred years of the history of Moldova. The various state formations attempted to assimilate the territory nationally and religiously and to socially engineer the population in order to integrate Moldova into new state systems; in this context, the loyalty of the population was always an issue.[74] As Dumitru and Negura point out, the models of "political governance and identification" were always "imported from the outside and were not an "autochthonous" production of the indigenous elites."[75] Indigenous Moldovan leadership emerged in the religious sphere in the form of charismatic monastic and peasant actors. In this article, I have briefly introduced two of them. Leadership amongst marginalized and colonized peoples during times of crisis often finds expression through religious charisma and possession cults in particular. Weber explicitly links the emergence of "charisma" to periods when there is a "suspension of the ordinary course of life" when crises or dramatic events need resolution. With "charisma" comes the "prophet" who works as a counterpoint to priestly "routinized" religion giving rise to sects and heterodox positions.[76] In vernacular Orthodox culture in Moldova, the potential for the emergence of such figures during times of crisis is enhanced by the availability and popularity of narratives that prophesize the intervention of divine and supernatural actors in worldly affairs.

Inochentie Levizor and Alexandru Culeac, the founders of Inochentism and Archangelism respectively, are significant characters as they succeeded in achieving a "decentering" of Orthodox authority through their bodily and visual cultural interventions. They established "liminal" movements that remained nominally within the Orthodox Church whilst critiquing contemporary Orthodox institutions and practices. The Orthodox Church in both Romania and Russia in the 20th century has a history of compromise and entanglement with state politics and power. The "liminality" of Inochentism and Archangelism arose at a time of extreme crises and change that has defied political resolution, just as the critique of Orthodoxy from its own margins also defies resolution.

What I term "liminal" Orthodoxies are those that, according to their own self-representation and self-identification, occupy a space of critique of the "Church of this world" from a marginal position that is focused on the next world and stands at the threshold of the End of Days. Liminality deals with what happens during times of passage, times of change, and times of crisis. In Orthodoxy, the structural relationship between magic and the popular miraculous, the prophetic agency of the monasteries, and the institutional priesthood presents a particular situation in which "liminality" is prone to take on a fluid permanency. Liminality has an innovative or generative quality that is in tension with an attachment to the familiar patterns, practices, and ways of being in the world that are more readily associated with folk religion.

In his discussion of contemporary western radical ecclesiologies, Henk de Roest opts for the category of "marginal" as a "nonjudgmental" term to describe those ecclesiologies "which have arisen out of, or are located on, the margins of mainstream (or 'traditional') churches." The narratives told by members of such groups "to articulate and justify their identity" are often excluded from discussions about the histories, identities, and trajectories of their mainstream counterparts.[77] One of the aims of this chapter is to stand as a corrective to these tendencies by demonstrating that groups that occupy the unsettling periphery and that transgress Orthodox boundaries can tell us much about the center ground from which they are excluded.

The idea that Christ or other divine or saintly persons have returned to earth and walk amongst us was not an Inochentist or Archangelist innovation; amongst radical and mystical Russian sects, starting with the Christ Faith in the 17th century, the bodily reincarnation of successive Christs and of the Holy Spirit, in both male and female in form, was at the heart of their radical beliefs.[78] The belief in human incarnations of divine persons is condemned in Russian Orthodoxy as the heresy of *chelovekoobozhanie*, "worshiping man"[79] and Inochentism came to be associated with this current of Russian mysticism.[80] I argue here, however, that the particular case of

20th-century Moldova, when the "liminal" phases of transition from one state to another and from one religious institution, calendar, and language to another became permanent, the conditions were right for the ultimate form of border crossing, between the divine and human realms, to manifest multiple times.

ACKNOWLEDGMENTS

I would like to thank Dumitru Lăpușneanu and Igor Cașu for their advice and support whilst conducting research in Moldova.

FUNDING

The research for this article was partly funded by a Royal Irish Academy mobility grant.

NOTES

1. The territory of the present-day Republic of Moldova has also historically been referred to as Bessarabia. For a fuller account of terminologies associated with the territory, see Charles King, *The Moldovans: Romania, Russia, and the Politics of Culture* (Stanford: Hoover Institution Press, 2000), 18–22.

2. For an outline of anthropological approaches to border lands, see Pamela Ballinger, "'Authentic Hybrids' in the Balkan Borderlands," *Current Anthropology* 54(1): 31–60 (2004).

3. Lavie and Swedenburg, as cited in Ibid., 31.

4. Árpád Szakolczai, "Liminality and Experience: Structuring Transitory Situations and Transformative Events," *International Political Anthropology* 2(1): 152 (2009).

5. Árpád Szakolczai, "Marginalitás és liminalitás: Státuszon kívüli helyzetek és átértékelésük," *Regio* 23(2): 25 (2015).

6. On Gagauzia, see James A. Kapaló, *Text, Context and Performance: Gagauz Folk Religion in Discourse and Practice* (Leiden: Brill, 2011); and on Transnistria, see Kimitaka Matsuzato, "Inter-Orthodox Relations and Transborder Nationalities in and around Unrecognised Abkhazia and Transnistria," *Religion, State and Society* 37(3): 239–62 (2009).

7. The Revised Julian Calendar was adopted by the Orthodox Churches of Constantinople, Alexandria, Antioch, Greece, Cyprus, Romania, Poland, and Bulgaria at a congress in Constantinople in May 1923. Russia along with Ukraine, Georgia, and Jerusalem rejected its introduction.

8. The lunar part of the calendar, used for the calculation of Easter, was rejected by all Eastern Orthodox Churches, which is why Easter is celebrated on the same day amongst all Orthodox churches.

9. D. Croitaru, "Pericolul stilismului și inochentismului din Basarabia," *Misionarul* 8(1–2): 120–21 (1936).

10. Diana Dumitru and Petru Negura, "Editorial: Moldova: A Borderland's Fluid History," *Euxeinos* 15/16: 3–8 (2014).

11. Szakolczai, "Marginalitás és liminalitás", 19–20.

12. For a full account of these territorial changes and the politics of rivalry between Romania and the Soviet Union, see Wim P. van Meurs, *The Bessarabian Question* (New York: University of Columbia Press, 1994); and King, *The Moldovans*.

13. See, for example, Nicolae Popovschi, *Istoria Bisericii din Basarabia în Veacul al XIX-lea sub Ruși* (1931; repr. Chișinău: Museum, 2000); Ion Nistor, *Istoria Basarabiei* (Bucharest: Humanitas, 1991); and Mircea Păcurariu, *Basarabia: Aspecte din Istoria Bisericii și a Neamului Românesc* (Iași: Trinitas, 1993).

14. King, *The Moldovans*, 1.
15. Agnes Horvath, "Mythology and the Trickster: Interpreting Communism," in A. Wöll and H. Wydra, eds., *Democracy and Myth in Russia and Eastern Europe* (London: Routledge, 2008).
16. Geza Vermes, *Jesus the Jew* (London: SCM Press Ltd., 1983), 58–82.
17. Geza Vermes, *Christian Beginnings: From Nazareth to Nicaea, AD 30–325* (London: Penguin, 2012), 2–3.
18. Ibid.
19. See, in particular, Mozes Gaster's works on and collections of Romanian popular literature and manuscripts: Mozes Gaster, *Literatura populară română* (Bucharest: Ig. Haimann, 1883); Mozes Gaster, *Studii de Folclor Comparat* (Bucharest: Editure Saeculum I. O., n.d.).
20. See Laura Jiga Iliescu, *Răsplata Paradisului: Filoane Livrești și orale ale Tradițiilor despre Blajini în Spațiul Românesc* (Bucharest: Editura Academiei Române, 2006), 18–37; and Kapaló, *Text, Context and Performance*, 117–53.
21. Gaster, *Studii de Folclor*, 162.
22. Florentina Badalanova Geller, *2 (Slavonic Apocalypse of) Enoch: Text and Context* (Berlin: Max Planck Institute for the History of Science, 2010), 3.
23. Ibid., 11.
24. Gaster, *Studii de Folclor*, 177.
25. See Ibid., 158–76 on the apocryphal legends: Apocalypse of the Mother of God (*Epistolia Maicii Domnului*) and Apocalypse of the Apostle Paul (*Apocalypsul Apostolului Pavel*).
26. See Ibid., 46–51; Éva Pócs, "'Lilith és kisérete': Gyermekagyas-démonoktól vedő ráolvasások Délkelet-Európában és a Közel-Keleten," in Éva Pócs, ed., *Magyar néphit Közép – és Kelet-Európa határán*, Vol. 1 (Budapest: L'Harmattan, 2002), 213–38; and Kapaló, *Text, Context and Performance*, 221–24.
27. On the cult of the Archangel Michael in Byzantine Orthodox tradition, see Ovidiu-Victor Olar, *Împăratul înaripat: Cultul arhangelul Mihail în lumea bizantină* (Bucharest: Anastassia, 2004).
28. Irina Paert, *Spiritual Elders: Charisma and Tradition in Russian Orthodoxy* (DeKalb: Northern Illinois University Press, 2010), 10.
29. Moldavia was the center of a spiritual revival in Orthodoxy in the 18th century. The Ukrainian-born monk Paisii Velichkovskii, who championed the use of patristic ascetic texts and the tradition of the Prayer of the Heart, was invited to lead a revival of monastic life in Moldavia by Prince Grigore III Ghica (1764–67 and 1774–77). The monasteries of northern Moldavia (Bucovina) and central Moldavia remain important centers of monastic ascetic practice.
30. Paert, *Spiritual Elders*, 12.
31. Ibid., 9.
32. Nicolae Popovschi, *Mișcarea dela Balta sau Inochentizmul în Basarabia* (Chișinău: Tipografia Eparhială – "Cartea Românească," 1926).
33. *În scurt viața și faptele Părintelui Inochentie de la Balta* (Bârlad: Tip. Const. D. Lupașcu, 1924).
34. J. Eugene Clay's article on Inochentism draws mainly on Russian language sources and, although it gives a generally reliable outline of events in the life of Inochentie, it fails to discuss questions of Inochentie's teachings and divine identity in any depth. See J. Eugene Clay, "Apocalypticism in the Russian Borderlands: Inochentie Levizor and his Moldovan Followers," *Religion, State and Society* 26(3): 251–63 (1998).
35. Emily B. Baran, *Dissent on the Margins: How Jehovah's Witnesses Defied Communism and Lived to Preach About It* (Oxford & New York: Oxford University Press, 2014).
36. Sergei I. Zhuk, *Russia's Lost Reformation: Peasants, Millenialism, and Radical Sects in Southern Russia and Ukraine, 1830–1917* (Washington, DC: Woodrow Wilson Center Press, 2004).
37. See Popovschi, *Mișcarea dela Balta*, 1–8; and Clay, "Apocalypticism," 253.
38. *În scurt viața*, 11.
39. Popovschi, *Mișcarea dela Balta*, 10–19.
40. Charles Clark, *Bessarabia: Russia and Roumania on the Black Sea* (New York: Dodd, Mead & Company, 1927), 108.
41. See Andrei T. Niculescu, *Balta Orașul Luminilor Transnistrene* (București: 'Bucovina' I. E. Torduțiu, 1941), Ion Nistor, *Istoria Basarabiei* (București: Humanitas, 1991); and V. Bâtca, "Biserică Ortodoxă și Spiritualitatea Românească în Basarabia Interbelică," *Luminătorul* 43(4): 14–21 (1999).
42. Popovschi, *Mișcarea dela Balta*, 23.
43. Grigorie Botoșăneanu, *Confesiune și Secte* (București: Tipografia Cărților Bisericești, 1929), 51.

44. Popovschi, *Mișcarea dela Balta*, 136.
45. Ibid., 137.
46. Ibid., 124.
47. Clay, "Apocalypticism," 261.
48. Ibid., 255.
49. V. S. Yakovenko, "Psikhicheskaya epidemiya na religioznoi pochve v Anan'yevskom i Tiraspol'skom yuezdakh Khersonkoi gub.," *Soveremennaya pskihiatriya* 5(3): 191–98 (1911); and V. S. Yakovenko, "Psikhicheskaya epidemiya na religioznoi pochve v Anan'yevskom i Tiraspol'skom yuezdakh Khersonkoi gub.," *Soveremennaya pskihiatriya* 5(4): 229–49 (1911) .
50. I. M. Lewis, *Ecstatic Religion: A Study of Shamanism and Spirit Possession* (London: Routledge, 1989).
51. Ibid., 26.
52. Popovschi, *Mișcarea dela Balta*, 142.
53. Ibid., 143.
54. Feodosia Chirica and Alecsandru Skvoznikov, *Conspecte pentru cursuri missionere norodnice de înfruntarea învățăturii cei minciunoase a lui ieromonahul Innochentie, alcătuite de missioneri-propoveduitori a eparhiei-protoiereul Feodosie Chirica și Alecsandru Timofevici Skvoznikov* (Kishinev: Eparhialnaya Tipografia, 1916).
55. Popovschi, *Mișcarea dela Balta*, 63–64.
56. Ibid., 151.
57. Antim Nica, "Viața Religioașă în Transnistria," *Transnistria Creștina* 2: January–June: 41 (1943).
58. Ibid., 47.
59. *În scurt viața*, 55–59.
60. Ibid., 54.
61. *Pre scurt viața și faptele Sfântului Părintelui nostrum Inochentie de la Balta sau Evanghelia Dreptății* (Chișinău: Editura Trei Crai dela Răsărit, 2010), 70.
62. Szakolczai, "Marginalitás és liminalitás," 19.
63. Per-Ame Bodin, *Language, Canonization and Holy Foolishness: Studies in Postsoviet Russian Culture and the Orthodox Tradition* (Stockholm: Stockholm University Press, 2009), 89.
64. *O vedenie ce s'a arătat în anul 1920* (Iași: Institutul de Arta Grafice "Versuri și Proză," 1924), 26.
65. Ibid.
66. *Vedeniile lui Grigore Culiac și pătimirile lui pentru mărturisirea venirii a doua a domnului Isus Hristos* (Iaș: Viața Românească S. C., n.d.).
67. *O vedenie*, 6.
68. *Vedeniile lui Grigore Culiac*, 5.
69. A. Alexandrov, *Propovăduitorii Obscurantizmului (esența reacționară a sectelor religioase ale inochentiștilor, iehoviștolor și murașkoviților)* (Chișinău: Editura de Stat a Moldovei, 1958), 22.
70. *O vedenie*, 26.
71. I. Shvedov, " Кареьра архангела михаила," *Советская культура*, 4 April 1959, 3.
72. V. Pasat, *Pravoslavie v moldavii: vlast' cerkov' verujushhie 1940–1953, 1953–60* (Moskva: Rosslen, 2009), 200.
73. Reports of their illegal border-crossing activities can be found in the press in the interwar period, see, for example, "Apostolul Inochentiștilor Face Spionaj?," *Informația*, 10 September 1937.
74. Dumitru and Negura, "Editorial," 3–4.
75. Ibid., 3.
76. Árpád Szakolczai, *Reflexive Historical Sociology* (London: Routledge, 2000), 12–13.
77. Henk de Roest, "Ecclesiologies at the Margin," in Gerard Mannion and Lewis S. Mudge, eds., *The Routledge Companion to the Christian Church* (New York: Routledge, 2008), 251–71.
78. Zhuk, *Russia's Lost Reformation*, 15.
79. Laura Engelstein, *Castration and the Heavenly Kingdom: A Russian Folktale* (Ithaca & London: Cornell University Press, 1999), 51.
80. Botoșăneanu, *Confesiune și Secte*, 51.

Fluid Identity, Fluid Citizenship: The Problem of Ethnicity in Postcommunist Romania

MARIUS ION BENȚA

This article aims at capturing a paradoxical situation of modern Romanian nationalism that is both a symptom and a consequence of the country's postcommunist "liquid" modernity: the tension between the essentialist and the constructionist discourses related to nationalism and ethnic identity. Approaching this topic can be an important endeavor not only for a better understanding of the condition of an eminently liminal geography in Europe's late modernity (East/West, democracy/totalitarianism, tradition/modernity) but also for addressing two questions of major importance to political anthropology: (1) Which are the political consequences of exposing a certain community to the scientific discourse produced in the sphere of the social sciences about that very community? (2) How is it possible for modern national identity to be commodified and for citizenship to be contractualized?

INTRODUCTION: CONFLICTING CONTEMPORARY DISCOURSES ON ROMANIAN NATIONALISM

The problems related to nationalism, national identity, and ethnicity are not only central to political anthropology but pose some of the most stringent and implacable problems to the social sciences in general. Perhaps the greatest difficulties associated with such topics arise from the fact that social scientists themselves can never escape being part of a nation, which is to say, first, that they may find it difficult if not impossible to set a distance between themselves and the object of their research and, second, that their scientific discourse can have serious, existential consequences for their daily life and the life of the society they belong to. In this article, I make use of the specific case of Romanian postcommunist nationalism to look into a more general and universally human problem: the conflict between the essentialist and the critical-constructivist discourses regarding Romanian nationalism. The question that I approach here is not which of the paradigms gives the right answer or which one brings more explanatory power. Rather, it is more important to investigate how it is possible that nationhood appears to be socially constructed to a distant observer while being experienced as an ineffable essence by its members.

The problem is complex and all the more so for the Romania context, which is a multiethnic and a fundamentally liminal space. For this reason, we need to restrict the present analysis to the particular question of Romanian nationalism while trying to understand a more general problem: the condition of nationalism in modernity. Space will not permit us to enter into interethnic problems in Romania or the nationalist discourse of the Hungarians living in Transylvania.

Romanians have always seen themselves as inhabitants of a land that lay in-between large tectonic plates: the Russian, Habsburg, and Ottoman empires, a condition that Sorin Alexandrescu called the "paradox of belonging,"[1] which he connected to two other paradoxical conditions of the Romanian nation: a temporal one, namely the absence of clear stages in the cultural history of Romania (such as the Renaissance or the Baroque eras), and a cultural one, namely the cleavage between the written culture of the elite and the oral culture of the vulgus. One can presume that this condition may be the root of a fundamental sense of permanent liminality shared by the inhabitants of this space regardless of their ethnic background, a sense that made them more permeable (or more vulnerable) to the permanentization of ambivalence and the expansion of fluid forms of identity brought about by the "liquid modernity," to use the words of Zygmunt Bauman,[2] and more prone to the alluring invitations from today's market fundamentalism, which tends to generalize the contractualized types of citizenship, as Margaret Somers has shown it.[3]

The consciousness of a particular ethnic group expresses itself in moments when an englobing empire falls apart. Such was the case of the Roman Empire in the fourth and fifth centuries, which allowed the multiplicity of traditions in Europe to become apparent or, later, when the Ottoman, Russian, and Habsburg empires left room for numerous national consciousness to become manifest in Eastern Europe. The Romanian nation is a latecomer on the stage of history, and it is in the end of 19th and the beginning of the 20th centuries that nationhood was constituted and national consciousness awakened.

After the fall of communism, both the media and the academic life in Romania were dominated by very vocal — often aggressive — debates when matters of national identity, interethnic relations, minority rights, and national unity were concerned. In the confusion of voices and ideas, one could discern two dominating poles, which I will call *essentialism* and *constructionism*[4] — and a wide range of discourses in between. To reach the problem that I intend to discuss in this article, let us present these poles briefly.

The first is what we might call the essentialist or substantialist camp of thinkers. These refer to national identity with reverence and in line with a Romantic, Herderian conception of the *Volksgeist*; they ground their discourse upon the writings of such thinkers as the philosophers Lucian Blaga — the one who developed a whole philosophy of the Romanian "matrix space" (*spațiul mioritic*),[5] Constantin Noica,[6] Petre Țuțea,[7] Nae Ionescu,[8] or Orthodox theologians, such as Dumitru Stăniloae[9] or Nichifor Crainic.[10] They seek to preserve and promote the Romanian language and traditional culture epitomized in the Romanian peasant, in the space of the traditional village, and the literary creations of the folk, such as the *doina*[11] or anonymous poetic creations, such as the ballad *Miorița*. They glorify the pantheon of significant Romanian heroes: historical, literary or political figures, such as Mihail Eminescu, the Romanian "national" Romantic poet, the prince Michael the Brave (*Mihai Viteazu*), the Dacian king Decebalus, and the Roman emperor Trajan. They seek to safeguard the Romanian national spirit against what they see as the moral corruption of the West and modernity in general or the European Union in particular. In the substantialist perspective, the essence of the Romanian identity is ineffable and impossible to grasp by a foreigner and tends to be associated with religious faith, notably Orthodox but also Greek-Catholic. In some discourses of ethnophyletist resonance, the Orthodox and Romanian identity are identical or at least inseparable; for instance, Nae Ionescu saw Romanian-ness and Catholicism as clearly incompatible realities.[12] They tend to ignore other ethnic identities living in Romania altogether or to consider them as being part of the Romanian nation — a view that legitimizes the "unitary and indivisible National State" expressed in the Romanian Constitution's First Article — and at times see ethnic minorities as part of the oppressive waves that have affected Romanians and still menace the country's territorial integrity.

Radical versions of essentialism have been accommodated during the interwar period by the far-right movement Iron Guard and, after 1989, by various Romanian trickster figures acting in the fields of politics or the arts, such as Corneliu Vadim Tudor (a far right political leader and a court poet of the *ancien régime*), Gheorghe Funar (a far right political leader and ex-mayor of the Transylvanian city of Cluj), George Becali (a far right political leader and businessman involved in football business), or Dan Puric (an actor and essayist), whose ideas fall under a specific form of Romanian exceptionalism concerned obsessively with the greatness of the Romanian nation and the Dacian origin of the Romanians. Their discourse has been labeled using such pejorative terms as "romanianism" (*românism*) or "dacopathy" (*dacopatie*).

Foreign anthropologists or historians who had done extensive research in Romania, such as Katherine Verdery,[13] Gail Kligman,[14] Claude Karnoouh,[15] Dennis Deletant,[16] or David Kideckel,[17] were able to regard the object of their study without passionate involvement, and they tended to look at the essentialist perspective with the eyes of the curious but detached scientist; to Romanian intellectuals, such a position is difficult to adopt, and those who decided to choose alternative approaches did it often as an equally passionate enterprise of disenchanting, deconstructing, or merely rejecting the essentialist discourse, which they treated either with candor or with contempt. One can mention in this camp the philosopher Horia Roman Patapievici,[18] the historians Lucian Boia[19] and Neagu Djuvara,[20] or representatives of the young left in contemporary Romanian academia. Such thinkers seek to bring a breath of fresh air over the stale conception of Romantic substantialism by questioning the validity of essentialist concepts by subverting the founding myths and the grand narratives of the Romanian nation[21] and by drawing unmitigated portraits of national heroes. Put simply, nationhood for them is neither given nor essential but dynamic and socially constructed through discourse and cultural practices and reducible to a set of constitutive elements and simple mechanisms.

It is important to note that some Romanian thinkers cannot be easily located along this conceptual axis, even though most of them — such as the best-selling philosophers Andrei Pleşu or Gabriel Liiceanu — excel at criticizing, deploring, or deriding the flaws and blemishes of the Romanian *geist* and look at Romanian national identity with both love and repulsion. There are also some interesting poles of discourse that have emerged in the multiethnic region of Transylvania, which appear to combine essentialist and constructionist viewpoints. One could mention here the "project-oriented" perspective of the sociologist Vasile Dâncu[22] — who diagnoses as pathological both the lack of a national project in postaccession Romania and the people's poor conceptualization of their future — and the "regional manifesto" of Sabin Gherman, a journalist who promotes a deconstructing work directed at Romanian nationalism with the aim of founding (or bringing to the surface) the essence of the Transylvanian identity, which presumably transcends the ethnic boundaries of the Romanian and Hungarian communities of Transylvania; his manifesto has generated many controversial reactions in the media.[23]

Politically, the discursive poles related to Romanian nationalism after 1989 are subjected to a certain ambivalence and vacillation rather than clear-cut options. What was commonly perceived as right in the political stage in Romania — the center-right parties of PNŢCD (*Partidul Naţional Ţărănesc–Creştin Democrat*, The Christian Democratic National Peasants' Party) and PNL (*Partidul Naţional Liberal*, The National Liberal Party) along with the far right movements tended to be associated with the essentialist discourse, whereas the traditional left side parties of PSD (*Partidul Social*

Democrat, The Social Democratic Party), PD (*Partidul Democrat*, The Democratic Party), or PSM (*Partidul Socialist al Muncii*, The Socialist Workers Party of Romania) — tended to place less weight on the nationalist component. This tendency changed in the 2014 presidential campaign, when the PSD candidate Victor Ponta abruptly made use of Romanian-ness and Orthodoxism as axiological pillars for his political discourse in his confrontation with the PNL candidate Klaus Iohannis, a Lutheran Saxon from Transylvania. It is unclear whether PSD is prepared to cultivate this "heritage" in the future, given that Victor Ponta lost that battle with Klaus Iohannis. The essentialist discourse resonates with similar discourses in other Eastern European countries and sometimes with Eurasianism, mostly as a reaction to what they perceive as the destructive mechanisms of the West and the European Union. However, some of the luminaries of the "young left" movement in Romania, who are largely environmentally active and antiglobalists, also share some of the aims and critical standpoints of the Eurasian doctrines.

AN EPISTEMOLOGICAL PARADOX

To try to understand the relationship between the two main viewpoints related to nationalism is important not only for the case of Romanian nationalism but for elucidating the problem of national identity in general, which may be one of the most important problems of political anthropology. Indeed, any nationalism can be seen from this double perspective, which leads one to a paradoxical situation when one tries to understand the problem of a plurality of nations coexisting in a given territory and being aware of each other.

Essentialism is a discourse about the nature and character of national identity. Constructionism, in this case, is a discourse about how essentialist identity *appears* to be constructed. The essentialist discourse belongs to the sphere of the lived experience of the person who identifies as a member of a specific nation. The constructionist discourse belongs to the sphere of anthropology. Obviously, we are not talking here of two independent spheres of life, because one makes the object of the other, which is to say that one is aware of the other. However, this "relationship of awareness" is not reciprocal, or at least not at the same level.

We can formulate now the main question of the present article: What happens when a scientific "construct," such as a conception on the social construction of national identity, is being "thrown back" to the people whose lives are founded upon an essentialist identity and who have never questioned the solidity of their own experience of nationhood? In the words of phenomenological sociology, we need to ask ourselves what happens when individuals in the "natural attitude" are being exposed to a (deconstructing) scientific discourse about themselves. Is it legitimate for academic sophistication to be "poured out" over human beings? Does the scientist have the right to subvert their identity?

We have to deal here with two separate spheres of experience and two different *attitudes*: the *scientific attitude* and the *natural attitude*. Alfred Schutz, the founding father of phenomenological sociology, analyzed the relationship between the sphere of everyday life and the sphere of science using his original conception of the "finite provinces of meaning."[24] Human life, Schutz said, is experienced as a series of passages between provinces. Everyday life is just one province among others, such as the world of drama, the world of fiction, the world of science, the world of religion, the world of dreaming, and so on. Provinces are, to a certain extent, autonomous and consistent in themselves but incompatible with each other. Schutz's main concern was to understand the way knowledge and experience get transferred from the province of everyday life into the world of science — particularly the social sciences — as his main objective was to establish an epistemological foundation for the social sciences. However, the problem of projecting back the output of the world of the social sciences onto the world of daily life, which is crucial for understanding the life of modern nationalism, was not addressed by Schutz.

Most likely, the immediate answer to our question would be that, in the case of an individual or a community exposed to a discourse that subverts their national foundation, one of the following outcomes are possible: (1) nothing happens, and identity stays the same; (2) a crisis of identity follows; (3) the essentialist identity is reinforced; (4) a sense of liberation is experienced, which may open the gate to a new identity.

Let us note that a form of social constructionism originated in the phenomenological sociology based on the writings of Alfred Schutz, Max Weber, and Edmund Husserl. This initial type of constructionism, which was based upon the phenomenological concept of bracketing (or *epoché*), was not conceived as a denial of reality but as a temporary bracketing intended for purely methodological purposes. This basis was later misunderstood or ignored, and this made it possible for various flavors of constructionism to turn into a nearly metaphysical discourse about reality by their claim that, by definition, reality is a (mere) social construction, that is, a manipulatable illusion. Obviously, this immediately prompted the need for social scientists to perfect their skills at constructing, deconstructing, reconstructing, subverting, and manipulating social reality.

"Sending back" identity theory to identity bearers is somehow similar to an act of psychoanalysis. It is a deconstruction work: One does not destroy a house but deconstructs it and dismantles it piece by piece, while retaining the knowledge related to how it was made, to its inner working and inner structure. One has disenchanted it. What can, or should, one do with this knowledge? From the epistemological standpoint of knowing reality (for example, identifying the founding myths of reality), one can turn to the standpoint of controlling, affecting, distorting reality and to the enterprise of murdering the founding myths of the nation.

Now, if national identity is socially constructed, which are its constitutive elements?

Several constructionist models have been conceived,[25] but here we will focus on a particular model of modern nationhood that exhibits a certain "mathematical elegance" in the sense that it somehow opens the door to algorithmic manipulations of national identity. The model was proposed by the Swedish anthropologist Orvar Löfgren.[26]

The paradox of modern nationalism lies in the fact that that nationhood is experienced in a timeless, ineffable way by the "innocent" members of the nation, and yet it is an invention of modernity strikingly similar in its structure, rituals, and cultural practices everywhere from the United States to Eastern Europe or China.

The constitutive ingredients of a nation are, according to Löfgren, the following: a set of symbols, such as the national anthem, the national flag, or the sacred texts; a common history, a set of sacred events of the past that are celebrated as holidays; a set of sacred places; a pantheon of heroes venerated by the members of the nation; a set of national values and styles of cultural expression.

This formula of nationhood permits one to investigate the congruence of the constitutive list of elements in the case of two communities presumably belonging to the same nation, such as Romanians from Romania versus Romanians from the Republic of Moldova or Hungarians from Hungary versus Hungarians from Transylvania. Do both communities venerate the same pantheon of "sacred figures"? Do they share their significant historical moments? Do they make use of the same symbolic equipment? Of course, knowing the formula of nation-construction also allows one presumably to alter, to subvert, or to reconstruct a nation, given that contemporary media provide us with powerful tools in this sense. Such "experiments" are, unfortunately, not limited to the sphere of imaginative thinking. A quick view at Romania's communist history shows us the huge dimension of the Orwellian "reconstruction work" that has been purposefully operated on by the constitutive elements of the nation: The memory of some significant figures was minimized or wiped out completely, while insignificant figures were pushed forward, historical events that the communist regime was uncomfortable with were eliminated from books, and the whole set of national values and symbols was distorted.

Were Romania's communist regimes efficient in their enterprise of reshaping the nation according to their own will? To a large extent, yes. All communist regimes were caught in the spiral of a never-ending revolution,[27] and all revolutionary powers sought to apply such engineering and reverse-engineering technologies upon their communities.

A WAY OUT OF THE CONUNDRUM

To find a way out of this paradoxical situation, one must try and regard the problem from a wider perspective, and we will evoke here some of the ideas of Eric Voegelin,[28] Hans Morgenthau,[29] Arpad Szakolczai, and Agnes Horvath,[30] among others.

First, let us note that merely studying the structure of a biological organism and being able to describe its organs and anatomy does not give us the ability to make a living being, to create life. At best, one can gain enough knowledge to destroy that living being more quickly or more efficiently. So too, describing the recipe of identity or being able to deconstruct it does not make us able to create a living identity, only, at best, an image of it, a dead replica. If a national identity cannot exist without a constitutional recipe embedded in a political theology, it does not mean that an empty theology or an empty recipe devoid of spiritual connections can replace or create a nation altogether.

Nationalism was an invention of modernity just like any other "-ism," (modernism, atheism, liberalism, positivism, fascism, or communism) as Voegelin calls them, because it was the result of a cascade of exported revolutions starting with the Enlightenment and the French Revolution and continuing with the Napoleonic Wars and the spread of the Wilsonian principles in Europe, which opened the way to the liberation of smaller nations from the domination of empires, as Morgenthau put it.[31] Nationalism is experienced in an essentialist mode by its adherents, because it imposes itself upon them in the form and with the power of a religion. For this reason, it must be seen and treated like a religious phenomenon in a multireligious world, an inner-worldly religion that has lost its transcendental orientation. The nation has slowly replaced God, turning traditional religion into a new form of practice that involved worshipping the nation, initially *along with* the Divine, then *instead of* the Divine. The main consequence of this was the axiological free-floating of the community. A nation was thus found to be valuable and sacred by itself, not by being rooted in the Divine. Breaking the connections between nationhood and transcendence, which was a process similar to the unanchoring of a ship or the disconnection of monetary value from gold that took place in 1971, must be seen in tandem with other significant "disconnecting" moments in the genesis of modernity, such as the 18th-century conceptions that evolution and order can occur "spontaneously" and independently of a designer, as Harald Wydra has shown it.[32]

All the socially engineered productions of modernity of gnostic inspiration, such as the Marxian socialist new man, are "golems."[33] So too are modern nations, which have been constructed alchemically in the 19th century, once the large empires collapsed, and the orientation towards transcendence shifted into an orientation towards an immanent object of worship: the nation. This explains how it is possible for Romanian nationalists to identify nationhood with Orthodoxy in spite of the fact that the Romanian nation's unity project has resulted largely from the work of two liminal actors: a liminal denomination, the Greek Catholics of the Transylvanian School (*Şcoala Ardeleană*), situated at the frontier between Orthodoxy and Catholicism, and a liminal ruler, King Ferdinand, the son of a foreign king who had accepted the Romanian crown and conversion to the Orthodox faith.

Nationalism as an international ideology does not entail a flattening out of identities, as was the case in many empires, but rather the use of a structural model composed of replaceable elements. Such an invention was triggered by a movement of *corruption* that has been affecting the West for many centuries. Voegelin identifies the genealogical source of this degrading tendency in Gnosticism seen as a long-term project of autonomy of the human being developed in parallel with, and probably as a response to, Christianity.

Even in the most secular, "desacralized," and modern societies, Mircea Eliade says, human beings rarely display a truly "nonreligious" attitude,[34] as "they sometimes stagger under a whole magico-religious paraphernalia." The glorification and veneration of one's collective identity can be easily identified as such a type of camouflaged religion. Therefore, one can say that modern nationalism manifests itself in the form of a plurality of secular (or inner-worldly) religions in the Voegelian sense of the word,[35] a multiplicity of cults increasingly aware of one another, in the words of William Stoddart[36] or Seyyed Hossein Nasr[37] and, one could add, bound to coexist like a Westphalian brotherhood struggling for mutual acceptance under the revolutionary dream of freedom, equality, and fraternity.

But what kind of brotherhood can one have in a world where the traditional figures of authority have been abolished and "love" has been substituted with its secular counterparts "solidarity" and "altruism,"[38] a feeling that is always ready to turn into class struggle?

Modern nationalism lives in the spirit of the postmodern condition, which is eminently liminal and invites one to obey norms and to subvert them at the same time; it is that spirit of political correctness and mutual tolerance that resembles an airport's multifaith prayer room that was designed to accommodate both Christians and Satanists.

This can only be a "brotherhood of man without a father," in Voegelin's words,[39] that is, a Westphalian "brotherhood of orphans" revolving in the reel dance of a never-ending revolution.[40] The alchemical process is never completed, because it is the very logic of any Voegelian "-ism" and, indeed, the very logic of modernity, to be caught in a permanent making and remaking of itself, thus, to be driven into a state of permanent liminality, as Szakolczai theorized it.[41] Modernity — or rather the "-ism" that constitutes its backbone, *modernism*—shares this paradoxical link with the two great waves of totalitarian regimes that have swept the last century, communism and fascism, as Horvath noted.[42]

The self-engineering character of permanent liminality manifests itself in the models of modern national governance through *constant reform*. Social reform is the product, says Morgenthau,[43] of liberal philosophy's belief in the transformative power of reason. Social or economic problems are always solvable by human intervention, by introducing a new piece of legislation, by constantly adjusting the system through smart policies: Indeed, the excess of emergency ordinances in post-1989 Romania makes the country appear as living in a state of permanent emergency. This is the very same logic that helps any trader to operate on the free market of secular liberalism.

Rationalism, modern science, magic, and alchemy belong to the same realm of human activities that emerged out of the same attitude that originated in the rejection, questioning, or attempting to dominate the given order of the world, as it has been noted by such authors as Morgenthau,[44] Gell,[45] or Horvath.[46] Therefore, modern politicians are like magicians who promise they will perform all the appropriate tricks in order to solve any problems. All the legal experiments in the name of science and the faith in its positive mission are but forms of magic and theurgy.

Is there a "next stage" of this never-ending work-in-progress? Orientation towards the future, the project, "the next level," and "the next version" is indeed the obsessive drive of modernity, which appears to be a contest in engineering and self-engineering. Corporations, organizations, communities, and individuals excel at engineering and forging their lives for best results and for highest achievements with an unprecedented faith in algorithms and quantitative evaluations of performance or risk. Positive psychology, enterprise development, career development, team work, physical workout, beauty contests, science grant competitions, and the efforts to constantly advance the state of the nation, all glorify the ego and its technologies of self-engineering. As some sociologists celebrate the advent of algorithmic cultures,[47] one can realize that ethnicity and nationhood, too, have turned into industrial products generated and controlled algorithmically. But the overuse of quantitative procedures and algorithms in more and more areas of social life and human existence was shown to have harmful effects upon people.[48]

So what exactly are we left with once the "second unanchoring" — the deconstruction of nationhood — takes place?

The German sociologist Ulrich Beck[49] believed that being together in this late modernity is no longer based upon faith in (or fear of) the Divine nor upon loyalty for one's nation or for one's family. The essence of being together is the *fear* of the unfortunate events of a disorderly future. Modernity has slowly lost the principle that works in traditional communities, where being together finds its essence in the graceful order of history;

instead, communities find their political force of cohesion, as Horvath put it, only in common suffering in a culture of fear.[50]

The art of fighting risk by minimizing it is done in modernity using the magic of numbers and statistics. Nicholas Taleb[51] has listed some of modernity's problems caused by overconfidence in planning and risk analysis, which arise from the fact that, by minimizing the probability of rare unfortunate events, we also minimize the probability of rare fortunate events. The history of mankind took place mostly through rare events, which have a deep formative effect upon individuals or communities. To use the words of Szakolczai,[52] one can say that the excess of planning and systemic adjustments is a way of chasing *grace* away from the life of society.

Risk is the fundamental element in the logic of mercantile behavior. Traders, investors, and banks seek to minimize risk and to maximize profit. Nationhood and nationalism were permeable to this mode of thinking and expression because of the contractualized understanding of national identity and citizenship, which prevailed in modernity and which originated in the ideas of the Enlightenment, such as Jean Jacques Rousseau's conception of the social contract. Naturally, a contract involves the idea of a basic exchange, of trading some of one's rights or possessions and of gaining others.

A closer look at the forms inhabited by contemporary Romanian nationalism shows that the "next level" in the general history of modern nationalism that results from constructionism being poured over the genuine, "zero-degree" experience of nationalism is our fourth hypothesis: a sense of liberation and openness towards a new identity. The main indexical element here is commodification.

The constant unanchoring and devaluing of collective identity operated through deconstruction and subversion forces us to speak of "cloud nationalism," a symptom that is strongly visible in contemporary Romania. Nationality has been ungrounded just like money or computer data and turned completely into a relational unit that is floating freely over the market.

CONCLUSION

Some nations tend to behave more like networks of services and commodities than territorial entities. As a consequence of the "overlay" of constructionist subversive ideas upon essentialist beliefs in the natural attitude, Romanian national identity entered this logic of production and trade, where citizenship is a brand, the nation is a service-provider, immigration policies are techniques of scarcity production, and passports are credit documents that grant the freedom of a set of potential actions in the future. In this logic, national identity tends to be reduced to contractualized citizenship, to be materialized in the passport and to be located at the intersection of collective identity (manifested as nation and state) and freedom (manifested as a collection of rights). To commodify identity means to place it in the circuit of commerce and to make it an object of *trade* instead of a *gift*, to subject it to constant improvements by producing ever new versions of it, and to have complete confidence in the superhuman, self-regulating abilities of the market-god that has replaced the transcendental legitimation and anchoring of nationhood once reserved to the Divine.

The main consequence of this shift is that national identity has entered an inflationary spiral that can lead to insolvable problems, of which I will mention here two.

The first problem created by the commodification of national identity refers to the specific case of the "conflictualization" of liminal areas. Borderline communities, which tend to be marginal, multiethnic, and multiconfessional (yet not always liminal), such as Transylvania, Moldova, and Northern Ireland can become spaces of competing political theologies of nationhood where the inflationary logic can affect their balance, turning them into really liminal areas.

The second problem refers to the fact that the commodification of identity and citizenship leads to unsettling questions, such as "For whom would you die?" The problem surfaced in Romanian media in the context of the Ukraine war, when some political leaders warned of a certain risk for the conflict to spread to other countries. In a state of war, a young man's commitment to his nation is expected to go beyond all values and to accept to give his life for his country. Can one die for one's nation when one knows that national identity is socially constructed?

NOTES

1. Sorin Alexandrescu, *Paradoxul român* (Bucharest: Universul, 1998).
2. Zygmunt Bauman, *Liquid Modernity* (Cambridge: Polity Press, 2000).
3. Margaret R. Somers, *Genealogies of Citizenship: Markets, Statelessness, and the Right to Have Rights* (Cambridge: Cambridge University Press, 2008).
4. For the set of conceptions that see reality as "socially constructed," I prefer to use the word "constructionism" instead of "constructivism," because these theories have nothing to do with the adjective "constructive" and its meaning of "positive" or "valuable," but with the conception that social reality is not given as a transcendental essence but is constructed in intersubjectivity.
5. Lucian Blaga, *Spațiul mioritic* (1944; repr., Bucharest: Humanitas, 1994).
6. Constantin Noica, *Pagini despre sufletul românesc* (Bucharest: Humanitas, 1991).
7. Petre Țuțea, *Între Dumnezeu și neamul meu* (Bucharest: Fundația Anastasia, 1992).
8. Nae Ionescu, *Roza vînturilor* (Bucharest: Editura Roza vînturilor, 1990).
9. Dumitru Stăniloae, *Poziția domnului Lucian Blaga față de creștinism și ortodoxie* (Paideia, 1993); Mihail Neamtu, "Between the Gospel and the Nation: Dumitru Staniloae's EthnoTheology," *Archaeus* 10(3): 7–44 (2006).
10. Nichifor Crainic, *Ortodoxie și Etnocrație* (Bucharest: Albatros, 1997).
11. A specific form of a slow, melancholic song.
12. Ionescu, *Roza vînturilor*, 194–214.

13. Katherine Verdery, *National Ideology Under Socialism: Identity and Cultural Politics in Ceaușescu's Romania* (Berkeley/Los Angeles/London: University of California Press, 1991).
14. Katherine Verdery and Gail Kligman, *Peasants under Siege: The Collectivization of Romanian Agriculture, 1949–1962* (Princeton, NJ: Princeton University Press, 2011).
15. Claude Karnoouh, *Inventarea poporului-națiune* (2008; repr., Cluj: Idea Design & Print, 2011).
16. Harry Hanak and Dennis Deletant, eds., *Historians as Nation-Builders: Central and SouthEast Europe, Studies in Russia and East Europe* (London: Palgrave Macmillan UK, 1988).
17. Joel Martin Halpern and David A. Kideckel, "Anthropology of Eastern Europe," *Annual Review of Anthropology* 12: 377–402 (1983).
18. Horia Roman Patapievici, *Omul recent* (Bucharest: Humanitas, 2001).
19. Lucian Boia, *De ce este România altfel?* (Bucharest: Humanitas, 2013); Lucian Boia, *History and Myth in Romanian Consciousness* (1997; repr., Budapest: Central European University Press, 2001).
20. Neagu Djuvara, *Între Orient și Occident: Țările române la începutul epocii moderne* (Bucharest: Humanitas, 1995).
21. Karnoouh, *Inventarea poporului-națiune*; Mihai Stelian Rusu, "(Hi)story-Telling the Nation: The Narrative Construction of Romanianism in the late 19th Century," *Journal of Comparative Research in Anthropology and Sociology* 5(1): 101–120 (2014).
22. Vasile Dâncu, *Patrie de unică folosință* (Bucharest: Rao, 2010).
23. Géza Szőcs, ed., *M-am săturat de România! Fenomenul Sabin Gherman în viziunea presei* (Cluj: Erdély Hiradó/Curierul Transilvan, 2000).
24. Alfred Schutz, "On Multiple Realities," *Philosophy and Phenomenological Research* 5(4): 533–76 (1945).
25. Helen Ting, "Social Construction of a Nation – A Theoretical Exploration," *Nationalism and Ethnic Politics* 14(3): 453–82 (2008).
26. Orvar Löfgren, "Modernizing the Nation – Nationalizing Modernity," *Etnolška tribna* 15: 1–115 (1992).
27. Árpád Szakolczai, "Communism in between Myth and Reality," in Alexander Wöll and Harald Wydra, eds., *Democracy and Myth in Eastern Europe* (Regensburg, 2002); Ágnes Horvath and Szakolczai, *The Dissolution of Communist Power: The Case of Hungary* (New York/Abingdon: Routledge, 1992).
28. Eric Voegelin, *Modernity Without Restraint: The Political Religions, The New Science of Politics, and Science, Politics, and Gnosticism* (Columbia, MO: University of Missouri, 1999); Eric Voegelin, *Science, Politics, and Gnosticism* (1968; repr., Washington: Regnery Publishing, 2004).
29. Hans J. Morgenthau, *Scientific Man versus Power Politics* (London: Latimer House, 1946).
30. Agnes Horvath, *Modernism and Charisma* (Hampshire: Palgrave Macmillan, 2013).
31. Morgenthau, *Scientific Man versus Power Politics*, 53.
32. Harald Wydra, *Politics and the Sacred* (Cambridge: Cambridge University Press, 2015), 62.
33. Voegelin, *Modernity Without Restraint*, 280.
34. Mircea Eliade, *The Sacred and the Profane: The Nature of Religion* (New York: Harcourt Books, 1957), 204–207.
35. Voegelin, *Modernity Without Restraint*, 33.
36. William Stoddart, *Remembering in a World of Forgetting: Thoughts on Tradition and Postmodernism* (Bloomington: World Wisdom, 2008), 62.
37. Seyyed Hossein Nasr, *The Essential Seyyed Hossein Nasr* (Bloomington: World Wisdom, 2007), 1–20.
38. Voegelin, *Modernity Without Restraint*, 296.
39. Ibid.
40. Horvath, *Modernism and Charisma*, 107–114.
41. Árpád Szakolczai, *Reflexive Historical Sociology* (London/New York: Routledge, 2000); Árpád Szakolczai, "Living Permanent Liminality: The Recent Transition Experience in Ireland," *Irish Journal of Sociology* 22(1): 28–50 (2014).
42. Horvath, *Modernism and Charisma*, 133–137.
43. Morgenthau, *Scientific Man versus Power Politics*, 26.
44. Ibid., 79.
45. Alfred Gell, "Technology and Magic," *Anthropology Today* 4(2): 6–9 (1988).
46. Horvath, *Modernism and Charisma*, 44–48.
47. Robert Seyfert and Jonathan Roberge, eds., *Algorithmic Cultures: Essays on Meaning, Performance and New Technologies* (London: Routledge, 2016).

48. Cathy O'Neil, *Weapons of Math Destruction* (New York: Random House, 2016).
49. Ulrich Beck, "The Cosmopolitan Perspective: Sociology of the Second Age of Modernity," *British Journal of Sociology* 51(1): 79–105 (2000).
50. Horvath, *Modernism and Charisma*, 155.
51. Nassim Nicholas Taleb, *The Black Swan: The Impact of the Highly Improbable* (New York: Random House, 2007).
52. Árpád Szakolczai, *Sociology, Religion and Grace: A Quest for the Renaissance* (London: Routledge, 2007).

Central Marginality: Minorities, Images, and Victimhood in Central-Eastern Europe

ARVYDAS GRIŠINAS

The article discusses from an anthropological point of view the reasons why minorities tend to find themselves at the center of tensions in Central-Eastern Europe. It presents an idea that the answer to the question lays in the "human side" of the regional politics. In human experiential terms, the political "character" of the region and the image of ethnic minorities as political phenomena are both grounded in memory of suffering and victimization. Because of the historical and experiential circumstances, it became a basis for identity formation, perpetuating the regional tensions. However, such victimized identity can be hijacked and abused both by the actors themselves and the external forces.

INTRODUCTION

Ethnicity and minority-related political tensions in Central and Eastern Europe have been an emblematic topic in studies of nationalism since the collapse of the Soviet Union. Identity, whether cultural or political, ethnic or national, has become the semantic axis for these tensions. This is even understandable, since, after the collapse of the Soviet Union, the region had to redefine its presence in numerous spheres of life, including the political, cultural, and religious as well as the demographic and territorial. Most regional interstate or intrastate conflicts in one way or another resonate the theme of identity. In many cases, the tensions are closely related to ethnic minorities as these present the newly formed status quo with challenging dilemmas, not only regarding integration but also their own existential and legal integrity.[1]

This article will discuss from an anthropological point of view the reasons why minorities tend to find themselves at the center of regional tensions. It will present a theoretical sketch of an idea and illustrate with examples a claim that the explanation to this phenomenon can be found in understanding the "human side" of the regional politics. It will be argued that in human experiential terms, the political "character" of the Central-Eastern Europe and the image of ethnic minorities as political phenomena have a common pertinent sense of suffering and victimization. However, because of the region's history and human experience, this element plays more than a sentimental role. It in fact works as a basis for identity formation, perpetuating the regional tensions.

Victimhood-based identity here emerges at the same time as a factor that is central (identity-forming) and marginal (based on a victimized image and negative memory) in the regional politics. It provides the regional states and actors with a potent yet volatile identity narrative. It will be demonstrated how such victimized political climate perpetuates different schismatic processes in the regional politics, including the ethnic-minority-based tensions, image forgery, and perpetuation of political crisis.

Therefore, a possible way of diffusing these tensions is via solving the rooted "scapegoat mechanisms" in the region, as introduced by René Girard. This article does not try to give any definite policy suggestions. The point to be made here is different: The path to transcending the situation in Central and Eastern Europe is via articulating it differently. The article uses certain anthropological conceptual tools, such as *liminality* or *political images*, as well as René Girard's theory on victimhood and victimization. In doing so, it emphasizes the problematic human experiential core that perpetuates the tensions in the region discussed: the centralization of marginality in times of liminal transition and identity formation.

Ethnic minorities in the article are articulated as political images used in the public debate, and not the minorities themselves. The different peoples that are labelled by the term are too complex in their social and cultural structures and substances to conceptualize adequately. Instead, images of these peoples are created and used in political practice, on their turn eventually substantiating the identity through reciprocation of these images. It will be assumed here, therefore, that ethnic and political identity is a mixture of both essence and construction. This suggests that one is not antithetical to the other, but rather that conceiving political reality through images is part of the human condition and is emphasized in particular circumstances of lived fluidity and ambivalence inherent in the region.

Finally, the article will further cover the relation of the image of a minority to victimhood as well as scapegoating mechanisms.[2] It will be shown how anthropological theoretical concepts such as *liminality* and *political images* can be of use in understanding this dynamic in ethnic and national politics in Central and Eastern Europe. They can offer both new ways of understanding political identity as well as the issues related to ethnic minorities. Finally, and most importantly, they allow for understanding the emotional rootedness of the images of "Central-Eastern Europe" and "ethnic minority" in human experiences connected to victimhood as well as contemporary political worldview.

CENTRAL-EASTERN EUROPE AS THE MARGINAL CENTER

According to Girard, what he calls "sacrificial mechanisms" tend to emerge and are perpetuated when societies encounter crises. Their paradoxality is that. It is in this situation that scapegoating becomes central to the social or political process. It is used as means to diffuse the tension through blaming a third party for the social or political tensions at hand. The paradox here is that "The scapegoat is only effective when human relations have broken down in crisis, but he gives the impression of effecting external causes as well, such as plagues, droughts, and other objective calamities."[3] So the scapegoat can be blamed for virtually any reason, including historical destiny or political discontents. This is how the marginal becomes central to the entire process under circumstances when the course of things is out of one's control.

The area that broadly speaking, spans between Moscow, Berlin, and Belgrade, the ever-shifting and, in many respects marginal "grey area" between the eastern and the western worlds (or both at the same time) is a region that deserves to be articulated as a specific space with a particular political nature. To a large extent, this is a result of various historical processes, such as postimperial nationalism, Soviet demographic policy as well as traumatic experiences during the world wars and the Soviet occupation.[4] The region found itself at the margin but, most importantly, also at the center of the greatest civilizational developments. It was there that three of the major imperial powers (the Austrian-Hungarian, the Prussian, and the Russian) met and, having split and devoured the vast and in a way even central Polish-Lithuanian Commonwealth, ended. To each of them respectively, the region was marginal. Yet, it left a heavy imprint on future political identity formation in the region.[5]

Over the last century, it has experienced multiple crises, often finding itself at the center of the unfolding dramas, as a marginal and passive object instead of active subject. The region is central to the history of the 20th century. It was here that both the First and the Second World War began and where they left their most traumatic impact. And yet, paradoxically, it was marginal in that it had no role in deciding the Europe's future for the rest of the 20th century. This marginal character of the region along with violent and turbulent experiences during the world wars and Soviet occupation became the formative factor for regional political identities. In fact, identity-formation processes in the region have also been profoundly unstable. The end of the First World War gave rise to multiple localized modern nationalisms (including the Baltic States, Poland, and Hungary, among others).[6] This happened on a Lockean "clean slate," among the rubble of the Austro-Hungarian and Prussian empires. The outcome of the Second World War, however, imposed a systematic destruction of all these recent political self-articulations.[7] And during the Cold War, it was this area again that marked the ambiguous "buffer zone" between the Soviet and the Atlantic areas of influence, with the majority of states being communist yet not Soviet.

As a result, the violent and sacrificial element is recurrent in different local identity narratives across the region. Many Central-Eastern European states narrative-wise emerged due to the "sacrifices by the forefathers." Not only is this a result of the world wars but also the Nazi, Soviet, and local national, religious, and ethnic identity-related violence. Probably all national narratives in the region heavily rely on the sacrifices, often bloody, that people had made for the contemporary national status quo to appear. Divisions in the Balkans are a direct result of wars in the 1990s as well as the fracturing in the 19th century. Lithuania celebrates its blood sacrifices for independence from the Soviet Union, and Russia too has a sense of victimization deeply engrained, if not as a result of itself having suffered most from the Soviet regime, then in form of the mythological narrative of power once had and lost in imperial times.[8] The memory of these national sacrifices is then venerated via memorials, bank holidays, and political mythology.

Thus, another recurrent regional theme next to transitory marginality is identity, emerging out of this particular condition in which the region is. The fascinating element of this political reality is the importance of its symbolic, emotional, and associative political aspects. It is the images of national identity, historical heritage, and national pride among others that often overshadow even the pragmatic value of some political decisions in the region. And it is these topics that are fundamental to the articulation of an ethnic minority as well, often as scapegoats or dangerous "others" in times of crisis. Therefore, both are connected via being important and central to the local status quo and marginal or liminal in character at the same time. It is this element of centrality of the marginal that heavily influences the region's political character. This way a certain imaginary metareality emerges where the power play happens at the level of images. Otherwise, marginal images gain political power in times of ambiguity and become central for identity-related conflicts.[9] Therefore, there is some kind of relation or at least surprising coincidence between the character of central marginality and a minority.

THE HUMAN EXPERIENCE OF LIMINALITY IN POLITICS

But what is the source of such paradox? Ambivalence and mutability seem to be an ever-recurring theme in the region's history, dictating its "political character." The region is at the same time at the center and at the margin of the world that grew from the remains of the two Roman Empires. The binary dialectics and the limits of definition between the eastern and western Roman heritage, the Byzantine Orthodox and the Roman Catholic Churches, the Russian and multiple western empires, and the communist and the democratic worlds were always established with reference to this area. Therefore, the region itself has continuously remained "neither this nor that" — a minority at the center, "betwixt and between" of the two dialectically related worlds.[10]

Geographically it is often referred to as the transitory space. In the case of Ukraine, the state's name literally means "a land on the verge" or the "borderland."[11] Talking about the more recent history, it was and in some cases is still imagined as "in transition" from what can be broadly called "the Soviet existence" towards the liberal democratic existence, which nowadays becomes increasingly associated with the European Union. Most recently, it has been a clashing point between the new transformation of the civilizational binary mentioned above in form of the Transatlantic and what is becoming the trans-Asian worlds.[12] In Boris Yeltsin's words, the Cold War was replaced by the "Cold Peace."[13] The Central and Eastern European region became a field of different global power plays. It is an area of expansion for the North Atlantic Treaty Organization (NATO) and the European Union as well as an area of postimperial interest to the Russian Federation.[14] Ethnic minorities once again emerge here as a medium and a pretext for conflict, also used as a tool to justify power-interest-based politics.

Arnold van Gennep conceptualized and Victor Turner elaborated the conceptualization of the process of transition with the theme of identity at its center as *liminality*.[15] The term, as used by the authors, refers to small-scale tribal groups. Yet, it has been successfully applied by social and political thinkers in relation to contemporary politics as well, particularly when discussing paradoxical and ambiguous political realities.[16] Politics is most often considered a rational affair, where interests meet and clash, and strategies unfold, where negotiations happen and agreements are signed. However, there is another side, the a-rational one (one that is prereflective), which is of no less importance to lived political reality than the former. The "human side" of politics consists of passions, principles, historical narratives, images, and representations. And these become particularly important during liminal transitions. In short, politics is not only institutional, logical, and legal but also human, paradoxical, and experiential.[17]

Talking about recent experiential side of politics (including the effect on collective memory, narrative as well as political imaginary and culture) in Central-Eastern Europe, the Soviet Union realized a brutal modernization, particularly in the east of the region, which changed its face profoundly. It systematically destroyed and transformed the social, cultural, economic, political, and existential background, rendering the previous cultures, states, and societies into an ideologically uniform mass of modernist "Soviet people." In these terms, Sovietization meant a rapid shift from life as was given in any concrete context to a new, standardized Soviet one. The revolutionary nature of the Soviet narrative itself offered no settlement either, rendering the liminality permanent.[18] Life in the present "here and now" meant only a transitory state to the "real here and now" under communism, which never came.[19]

Instead, particularly under Brezhnev, it established a certain type of meaningless lived condition, a "society of boredom," where due to its transitory teleology no true lived existence is possible *yet*, but nothing changes *now* either.[20] Such purposeful liminal condition, coupled with an intrinsically if not explicitly violent policy inevitably invoked various corruptive experiences, prevalent in ambiguous situations, including rampant alcoholism, criminality, and displacement, which mark and are traditionally associated with the post-Soviet Eastern Europe.

After the Soviet "project" collapsed, these people once again found themselves in an ambiguous situation — deprived of their traditionally inherited past, the promised communist future as well as social and economic assuredness within the present. New political identities were formed (the states of Belarus, unified Germany, Ukraine, Moldova) and gained substance, and previously uniform identities split (Czechoslovakia, Yugoslavia) at precisely this time. The period resulted in multiple seemingly paradoxical events and processes. For instance, the Baltic States were the pioneers of the inner collapse of the Soviet Union, and yet, soon after regaining independence, they happily surrendered a part of their political and economic sovereignty to the European Union.[21] In the case of Czechoslovakia, the Czech and Slovak republics split and formed separate states peacefully as a result of "the rejection of the common state by the political leaders of the Czech majority."[22] It can be said that Ukraine had been experiencing its "post-Soviet revolution" as a rupture with the Soviet-style political mindset only recently. The efforts to "westernize" the Ukrainian politics, as it was conceived, started with the Orange Revolution and culminated with Maidan.[23] Belarus, in these terms can be said to still live under the circumstances of Soviet-imposed identity and power-logics.[24] The paradoxical combination of a loss of political orientation on the one hand and an almost dogmatic, intensive orientation away from the ambiguous presence, often "Westwards," on the other can be recognized as dominant throughout the region, neither of which are signs of experiential stability.

IMAGES OF ETHNIC MINORITIES AS METAREALITY

The fact that themes like identity, history, symbolism, and imaginary play a significant role in Post-Soviet politics, and particularly when talking about the problematic context of ethnic minorities, indicates the role that the "human side" holds in the region and the epoch. I would like to argue that this is because it contains an existential element. In a liminal state, where one's formal presence is continuously compromised and undergoes a permanent change, identity along with its signifiers become an existential rather than a nominal topic.

And this is the background for the tensions related to minority identities. Images that comprise a particular and fixed identity of an otherwise very ambiguous political reality, such as an ethnic minority, become a metareality when the former political structure and ways of interaction are subverted or otherwise existentially challenged (via *coup d'état*, invasion, large catastrophe, or other transgressive event). Experientially, similar to an Egyptian death mask, images become the only thing that remains true and stable for eternity.[25] They shift from representation to presence.

Hans Belting, an art anthropologist discussed the relation between the two in the case of religious iconography. According to him, in early Christianity, and later in the Orthodox Christian tradition the icons, the visual representation of the sacred images of saints (whose imaginary, symbolic status is the basis for the perception, if not the substance of their powers) actually constitutes their physical presence among the believers. Therefore, when an icon of a saint is being carried through the crowd in a religious demonstration, the effective result is the same as if a saint him- or herself would embody the picture and walk among the people instead.[26]

Ritualistic and quasi-religious political behavior is a very real part of the contemporary world. In human terms, the religious experience is a liminal situation, where the established limits (in this case, of the secular and the sacred) are transgressed or transcended. A similar transgression of the established political forms happens during a political crisis. Under such circumstances, the reality of an image (in the form of a mask, an icon, or a political image) becomes social reality. Next to various inauguration and official appointment ceremonies, there are national establishment celebrations, Independence Day commemorations, as well as other formal and informal political rituals, such as theatrical and symbolically charged revolutions or "occupy movements." These all establish images and identities, bring them into being and infuse them with political power.

René Girard describes a process how a scapegoat, a marginal social actor is blamed for the general crisis situation the society is in, but, through an act of sacrifice, they come to represent the liberation from the said situation. They become elevated and even worshiped as a result.[27] It is exactly at this moment that the marginal is put at the center of the social drama. A very similar motif can be recognized when analyzing different post-Soviet cases of political figure veneration cults or its opposite — the demonizing of an ethnic, religious, or other minority during political turmoil. Different images and identities are attached to the object in question, rearticulating their presence as well as the political situation in general. The image of a political or historical figure becomes the embodiment of the ideals of the nation.[28] The image of a certain historical period becomes the "true time," *illo tempore*, the golden age.[29] A certain minority, which previously, if articulated as different, was not inferior in any way, becomes a transgressor, even scapegoat for the ills of today, or a victim to be somehow protected or saved from the oppression of the majority.

This can be explained by the specificity of liminal experience. When profound changes in lived reality happen over a brief time, they transform both the context in which the lived experience takes place and the participants themselves. If the crisis situation is uncontrolled and large in scale, such as a war, a revolution, or a natural disaster, the perceived limits and forms of political reality diminish, creating an ambiguous and unclear experiential situation — an "Alice in Wonderland experience."[30] The sense that allows for discriminating what is real and fictional diminishes. This, for example, happened in cases of what was titled as "Donetsk and Luhansk Republics" in Eastern Ukraine, where the newly formed political entities were purely imaginary with no legal or political substance, yet, through people's participation in these political masks, as well as through outside "help for the suffering," they attained physical reality — they established governing bodies, passports, and municipal legal framework.[31]

Experientially, in such a transitory situation, rational assessment of the surrounding world becomes impossible due to its fluidity, in a way similar to when a person finds oneself in a dark and unknown space. Political imagination and will become the basis for articulating the surrounding reality as well as for the perception of the identity of elements that comprise it. In the contemporary world, such process is given many names, including propaganda, information wars, or, more recently, hybrid warfare. Through this ambivalent epistemological state, the image of an ethnic minority can thus become more potent politically than the minority itself.

For example, this was the case with the image of a Polish minority, mostly present in the Vilnius region in southeastern Lithuania. The minority itself, both linguistically and ethnically, is very mixed as a result of a long-term and close contact between the Poles, Belarussians, Russians, and Lithuanians in the region. A common self-title among the minority is *Tuteishi*, roughly translating as "the local people."[32] After the plane crash in Katyn in 2010, during which numerous Polish political figures, including President Lech Kaczyński and a number of senior officials of the Polish Armed Forces senior officials perished, the Polish-Lithuanian relations experienced a downfall.[33] In the context, and not without the initiative of some external interested parties, a Lithuanian Polish Party labelled the *Tuteishi* a Polish minority, encouraging nationalism-related internal disagreements. As a result, the leader of the party won a European Parliamentary election.[34] However, the important part is that all of this was done using historical, symbolic, and emotional argumentation with reference to an ethnic minority.

This way, questions regarding ethnic and national identities and political imagination become central not only in the post-Soviet Europe of the 1990s but also of today. With various large-scale political shifts taking place in the region throughout the 20th century, it was not only the objective state borders that fell and emerged between different ethnicities and nationalities causing tensions. Peoples' "life-worlds" or their perceived political reality changed as well, putting the population in new "dark rooms" again and again. As such, the post-Soviet condition required new imaginary articulations of themselves, the environment as well as the symbolical "others." As a result of human experiences in the 20th century, such a condition of liminal ambiguity became normative.

For this reason, the theme of ethnic minorities in the region is central: The image and its importance indicate the regional condition. Ethnic minorities are liminal in relation to dominant national identities in the same way as Central-Eastern Europe is liminal in relation to the western and the eastern worlds — via being "in between" the two, while at the same time remaining at the center of tension. On one hand, such presence provides an unknown and yet essential "zero point" from which the status quo draws its own identity. The presence of a minority or of a marginal "other" provides an opportunity for self-reflectivity and healthy renewal. At the same time, it is a marginal element that provides a certain dynamism of identity, which can be also destructive. Under liminal circumstances, the image can be used and shaped in different ways, allowing for multiple forms of abuse.

VICTIMHOOD AND IDENTITY

So what connects Central-Eastern Europe and the image of an ethnic minority, apart from its marginality, that exerts such possibly dangerous power? René Girard argues that the mode of social coexistence in the modern world is based on scapegoat mechanisms.[35] He shows how through the process of sacrifice, a ritualistic shedding of blood, the victim is being both marginalized and centralized. It is scapegoated and blamed as the cause of the negative situation that the society performing the sacrifice is in and is elevated as the medium to transcend the said situation — it becomes a sacred (as elevated by sacrifice) cult object, exerting considerable power at the same time. The liminal element here is that through the practice of sacrifice, the society itself transforms. Its identity incorporates the experience of sacrifice as central. Szakolczai demonstrates how even democratic identity can become grounded in victimhood and elevated suffering.[36]

We have already discussed the ritualist nature of especially post-Soviet politics. However, the bloodshed does not have to be ritualistic to be sacrificial. In the contemporary context, cases like post-Revolutionary France, articulating a "new society" based on the sacrifice of the old one, or Israel, articulating the prophesised haven from the prosecution of the Jewish nation can be mentioned, among others. Images of suffering, sacrifice, and victimhood figure constantly in memorials, national celebrations, and other artifacts of identity.

However, victimhood, and its paradoxical situation of being marginal and central at the same time does not have to entail bloodshed either. It can also be observed perhaps in any instance of marginalizing. The Holocaust and the post-Holocaust memory politics entail both — the marginalization and the cult thereafter. The image of Syrian refugees has become both the object for hatred and a media for the surfacing of righteousness in the Western world. Lesbian, gay, bisexual, and transgender groups are both an object for loathing and violent attacks and an iconic image for celebrating liberal values. The image of the "rich 1%" is both a popular marginalized scapegoat for all the late liberal ills and a representation of "success," as most recently evidenced by Donald Trump's US support in the 2016 presidential elections. In all these cases, the victimhood character of these *images* makes them central to the society in more or less liminal situations (the post-World War period, the Syrian Crisis, the contemporary crisis of liberalism, the US elections).

The same applies to ethnic minorities. An ethnic minority itself is often diverse and impossible to articulate. What is being manipulated at the political level is the uniform notion of a minority as an image. Emotionally, the image contains a sense of weakness, fragility, and, thus, victimhood. Similar popular images are children, mothers, endangered species, indeed post-Soviet States as the "third world," among others. If separated from the democratic discourse in which an effort, no matter whether successful or not, is made to "normalize a minority," the image on its own obtains a strong emotional charge — of compassion, the sense of injustice, as well as self-righteous judgement, invoking vows to defend from one side, and an often repressive or defensive response from the other, producing a conflict dynamics.

When this image is used as means to push political will, it may become a corrosive force with regards to a structure containing the minority or to the relations between the two states involved. This process can be observed in the long-standing contention between Hungary and Romania, which is centered on Transylvania, especially one of its regions in central Romania.[37] The region consists of a majority of Hungarian-speakers who call themselves *Székelys*. Politically, however they are nevertheless Romanians (as citizens of Romania), although seeking independence or at least autonomy for the region. A part of the minority as well as a significant amount of external interest are strongly advocating against the status quo, basing their arguments on historical and symbolical grounding. At the same time, a strong nationalist sentiment can be felt mixed with a sense of victimization, as the Hungarian-speaking Székely population feels its identity is being oppressed. An organization that is titled the Szekler National Council, in their website, while advocating the peaceful process of attaining autonomy, state (grammar unaltered, emphasis in the original):

> [It is] practically impossible to speak about the oppression of the Hungarian people in Romania, while the Orthodox expansion in even stronger, getting for this large amounts of money from the government, our children are forced to learn history and geography in Romanian language even in Hungarian elementary schools, there is no state university in Hungarian language for a community of aprox. 1,5 million people, paying taxes just like the Romanians, the army and police is almost 100% Romanian, even here, in Szeklerland, etc., etc. [...]
> It is very important to note, that our fight for the rights mentioned in these documents it was, and it is peaceful. We are aware, that for instance Kosovo gained independence using violence, and there are people nearby us, who are beginning to loose [sic] their patience. This is understandable, as long as almost every border in the region was changed in the last 20 years, only our wish for *not* an independent state, but only for an autonomous region is still pending, the state authorities don't even want to discuss about it. We are afraid, that this will lead to the appearance of other organizations, with more radical goals, and more radical way of act.[38]

Regardless of whether this is true or not, and whether the claims are justifiable or not, the position challenges the integrity of the modern status quo Romanian state, but, more importantly for us, the established image thereof, through emphasizing the sufferings of the Székely, which adds to the tensions between Hungary and Romania.

This example is relatively mild and does not involve Hungary acting particularly disruptively towards its neighbor. However, the recent Russian rhetoric and policy regarding protection of its image of "foreign ethnic minority" in many neighboring states, including Georgia, Ukraine, Estonia, and others, is different. The instance in Ukraine, with the quasi-rhetorical image of *Novorossiya* figuring in the center, can be seen as a prime example of forging an image, which through Russia's political action obtains real political power.[39] This introduces the *scapegoat mechanism* Girard talks about. The population of Russian-speakers in Ukraine is difficult to delineate. Some are born Russians but politically Ukrainians, others are culturally Russified ethnic Ukrainians, etc. However, the notion of a Russian minority as a universalized image and based on an imaginary political structure creates a special dynamics. On the one side, the "Russian minority" is represented as weak and victimized, that is, one that needs to be saved. This then justifies an emotionally invoked "defense" rhetoric. On the other hand, in a crisis state newly forged political identities, such as *Novorossiya*, the Luhansk National Republic, and Donetsk National Republic, are used to create a teleological justification for the "saving." In this instance, the materiality of the imaginary becomes a particularly potent means to push for a political agenda.

So, it is not the ethnic minority itself that is the corrosive force, rather the political-will-infused image that is applied to the minority through its quality of victimization. This way the victimized image of the minority becomes an interstate victimized entity, thus a certain schism is imposed between the status quo and the minority, which is then abused.[40] This way, the image of the minority can become a parasitic force, dividing the main political body through emotional extortion and victimization.

Therefore, historical suffering-based identity is the element connecting minorities to victimhood and conflict in Central-Eastern Europe, perpetuating related tensions. Through victimization, the often marginal and repressed situation of ethnic minorities becomes a central theme for these tensions, which makes the image of a suffering minority essential. It is important to note that it is the image rather than the minorities themselves that become the pretext for conflict as well as the means to project power. In this way, the imagery becomes a functioning part of the political and obtains real power.

CONCLUSION

This article started by asking the question why minorities-related tensions are a topical issue in the region as a whole. Through tracing the experiential side of political identity formation in the region we realized that it is because the image of an ethnic minority resonates the region's own existential condition. The condition can be briefly summarized through the idiom of "centralized marginality." The article then looked at the historical background for such a condition to emerge, discussing both the central and marginal situation of the region as a "borderland" from the late 18th century to the post-Soviet period. It was argued that, due to these particular circumstances, political identity becomes not only of nominal or legal but also of existential importance.

We then conceptualized the Central-Eastern European experience as "liminal" and inquired into the "human side" of politics in effort to understand this experience. Through discussing both Soviet and post-Soviet cases, the article argued that Central-Eastern Europe is in a situation where liminality becomes permanent. Politically, this means that political issues in the region are particularly susceptible to become hijacked and abused due to its numerous and ever-shifting political identities.

The article then demonstrated how under such regional dynamics, in liminal ambiguity, images and political ritualism became fundamental in establishing political presence. This grounds political identities, including those of ethnic minorities, on the human experiential political aspect discussed. This way the centrality of the marginal and ambiguous identity makes politics heavily symbolical and charged emotionally. As these emotional identities at the same time have existential weight and are so thoroughly ambiguous, they become a powerful political tool.

Finally, it was shown that images can become a corrosive force in politics. When grounded on an experience of suffering and victimhood, identities of ethnic minorities become symbolically and emotionally laden images. These images can and, in some cases, have become abused to justify both vindictive and repressive violence. Given the particularly ambiguous historical and political conditions in Central-Eastern Europe, this factor gains particular importance. Central-Eastern Europe itself, as a result of the geopolitical developments of the 20th century, became a metaphorical ethnic minority of the post-Cold War world on its own right. Through reciprocating the victimhood-based identity, it itself has become (and has been made) a marginal image in between the two worlds, both in need of help and a cause for conflict. The idea of marginal victimhood-based identity at the center of a conflict or tension can also help us understand other contemporary problematic regions.

NOTES

1. István Deák, "Uncovering Eastern Europe's Dark History," *Orbis* 51–66: 53–54 (1990).
2. Rene Girard, *Scapegoat* (Baltimore: The Johns Hopkins University Press, 1986).
3. Ibid., 43.
4. On the topic how the region became considered a borderland through an image of the East as well as on further dynamics of the image, see Tomasz Zarycki, *Ideologies of Eastness in Central and Eastern Europe* (London: Routledge, 2014).
5. Rawi Abdelal, "Memories of Nations and States: Institutional History and National Identity in Post-Soviet Eurasia," *Nationalities Paper* 30(3): 459–84 (2002).
6. While very similar traumatic and formative processes took place in South-Eastern Europe, particularly in case of Yugoslavia. Yet, there was another set of fundamental factors at play that this article is unable to expand upon, in particular — the religious contestation, the Islamic factor as well as the influence of the Ottoman Empire.
7. Yuri Slezkine, "The USSR as a Communal Apartment, or How a Socialist State Promoted Ethnic Particularism," *Slavic Review* 53(2): 414–52 (1994).
8. Russian sacrifice in the Soviet Union has been well elaborated upon in Geoffrey Hosking, *Rulers and Victims: The Russians in the Soviet Union* (Cambridge: Harvard University Press, 2006).
9. The Bronze Soviet Soldier statue in Talinn became a center for massive historical memory- and symbolism-based riots; "Deadly Riots in Tallinn: Soviet Memorial Causes Rift between Estonia and Russia," *Spiegel.de,* 27 April, 2007, http://www.spiegel.de/international/europe/deadly-riots-in-tallinn-soviet-memorial-causes-rift-between-estonia-and-russia-a-479809.html (accessed 30 Aug. 2016).
10. Victor Turner, *The Ritual Process: Structure and Anti-Structure* (New Brunswick: Aldine Transaction, 2008), 95–132.
11. The name appeared in the 17th century, when Ukraine was a part of the Polish-Lithuanian Commonwealth. However, the Russian imperial narrative has contested both the name and the notion by articulating it as the "Small Russia." See Serhii Plokhy, *The Origins of the Slavic Nations: Premodern Identities in Russia, Ukraine, and Belarus* (Cambridge: Cambridge University Press, 2006), 299–302.

12. Richard Sakwa, "Back to the Wall: Myths and Mistakes that Once Again Divide Europe," *Russian Politics* 1(1): 5 (2016).

13. W. Bradley Stock, "Special Operations Forces in an Era of Cold Peace," in Richard H. Shultz, Robert L. Pfaltzgraff, and W. Bradley Stock, eds., *Special Operations Forces: Roles and Missions in the Aftermath of the Cold War* (Darby, PA: DIANE Publishing, 1995), 29–45, 29.

14. This is peculiar, because Russia would probably be the last country to lack in territory or resources offered by the region. Therefore, to a large extent, it must be the sentiments — the nostalgia for the past, the fear of the West, the revanchist ideas, or perhaps most importantly the injured sense of pride and a particular self-vision—that pushes its expansive policy. Richard Sakwa argues that the annexation of Crimea was first and foremost a strategic step and a preventive policy against what Russia saw as a western expansive policy in form of Ukrainian "Kievite" nationalism. He also argues that Crimea has been a marginal area between Ukraine and Russia since the 1990s, administratively being in Ukraine but in many ways fostering Russian identity; Richard Sakwa, *Frontline Ukraine: Crisis in the Borderlines* (London: IB Tauris, 2015), 100–104. Either way, the fact is that identity — both of self and the other (the West) is constitutive for Russia's policy. It could seem surprising, but it is very typical that the source of the newest uprising of "Russian pride" becomes its imaginary margin, the "lost territories" in the West, instead of, for example, the established, uncontested, and unambiguous Central Siberia. "Russian pride" here is defined through the dialectics with the West, and the reference point once again becomes Central-Eastern Europe.

15. Turner, *The Ritual Process*, 95.

16. See, for example, Agnes Horvath, Bjørn Thomassen, and Harald Wydra, eds., *Breaking Boundaries: Varieties of Liminality* (Oxford: Berghahn, 2015); Bjorn Thomassen, *Liminality and the Modern: Living Through the In-Between* (Farnham: Ashgate, 2014).

17. Multiple paradoxes, especially related to political identity formation and nation-building can be understood through analyzing this part of public and political life. See Harald Wydra, *Politics and the Sacred* (Cambridge: University of Cambridge Press, 2015); and also Arvydas Grišinas, "Sanctifying the Political: Lithuania's Struggle Towards National Independence 1989–1992," in Kristóf Fenyvesi, ed., *Transition and Difference in East-Central European Context* (Budapest: International Association of Hungarian Studies, 2012), 121–29.

18. Thomassen, *Liminality and the Modern*, 93.

19. Árpád Szakolczai, *Reflexive Historical Sociology* (London: Routledge, 2000), 214–15.

20. On the "society of boredom," see Tomas Vaiseta, *Nuobodulio Visuomenė. Kasdienybė ir ideologija vėlyvuoju sovietmečiu (1964–1984)* [Society of Boredom, Ideology and the Everyday in Later Soviet Period (1964–1984)] (Vilnius: Naujasis Židinys – Aidai, 2014); Agnė Narušytė, *Nuobodulio Estetika Lietuvos Fotografijoje* (Vilnius: Vilnius Academy of Arts Press, 2008).

21. See Richard Mole, *The Baltic States from the Soviet Union to the European Union: Identity, Discourse and Power in the Post-Communist Transition of Estonia, Latvia and Lithuania* (London: Routledge, 2012).

22. Paal Sigurd Hilde, "Slovak Nationalism and the Break-Up of Czechoslovakia," *Europe-Asia Studies* 51: 649 (2010).

23. This shift in public political thinking was marked by an effort to (no matter how successfully) overrun the nomenclature and mafioso/oligarch-run power structure, inherent from the Soviet times, and, in its stead, to introduce a functioning legal and governmental system based on transparent democratic institutions. But, most importantly, it meant a rupture with the legacy and logics of Russia's dominance as a Soviet nexus-state over Ukraine via its former president, Viktor Janukovich. It was at the same time a political, economic, cultural, and mental shift.

24. More on this in Arvydas Grišinas, *Politics with a Human Face: Europe after Socialism* (London: Routledge, forthcoming).

25. Political ritualism and the role of identity in the process can be theorized anthropologically. Italian sociologist Alessandro Pizzorno, in his essay on the mask introduces the notion of a ritual mask not as something that hides the "true" identity of the wearer but rather as "another self," as something that embodies the ritual actor, a new identity within the social or political drama. Therefore, it can be said that one becomes someone politically (a soldier, a Russian, a socialist, or something else) through participation and practice (military training, participation in Russian life, living a socialist life). Alessandro Pizzorno, "The Mask: An Essay," *International Political Anthropology* 3(1): 5–28 (2010); see also Árpád Szakolczai, "Masks and Persons: Identity Formation in Public," *International Political Anthropology* 3(2): 171–91 (2010).

26. Hans Belting, *Likeness and Presence: The History of Image Before the Era of Art* (Chicago: University of Chicago Press, 1996), 1–14.

27. Rene Girard, *Scapegoat*, 90.

28. Raoul Girardet, *Politiniai Mitai ir Mitologijos* [Political Myths and Mythologies] (Vilnius: Apostrofa 2007), 84–117.

29. Mircea Eliade, *The Sacred and the Profane* (New York: Harcourt, 1959), 82.

30. Árpád Szakolczai, "Liminality and Experience: Structuring Transitory Situations and Transformative Experience," *International Political Anthropology* 2(1): 141–72 (2009).

31. "Ukraine separatists declare independence," *Aljazeera.com*, 12 May 2014, http://www.aljazeera.com/news/europe/2014/05/ukraine-separatists-declare-independence-201451219375613219.html (accessed 30 Aug. 2016).

32. The term was used to also title some inhabitants in Ukraine in USSR's 1931 census. Oxana Petrovskaya, "The Forming of Western Belarus Borderlands in 1939–1940," in Oleksandr Dyukov and Olesia Orlenko, eds., *Divided Eastern Europe: Borders and Population Transfer, 1938–1947* (Newcastle upon Tyne: Cambridge Scholars Publishing, 2011), 40–73, 45.

33. Viktoras Denisenko, "Penkios tezės Lietuvos ir Lenkijos santykiams [Five Theses for Lithuanian and Polish Relations]," *Geopolitika.lt*, 25 March 2013, http://www.geopolitika.lt/?artc=5941 (accessed 30 Aug. 2016).

34. See: Diana Janušauskienė, "Ethnicity as Political Cleavage: The Political Agenda of the Polish National Minority in Lithuania," *Nationalities Papers* 44(4): 578–90 (2016).

35. Wolfgang Palaver, *René Girard's Mimetic Theory* (East Lansing: Michigan State University Press, 2013), 135–94.

36. Árpád Szakolczai, "The Non-Being of Communism and Myths of Democratisation," in Alexander Wöll and Harald Wydra, eds., *Democracy and Myth in Russia and Eastern Europe* (London: Routledge, 2008), 55.

37. "Hungary and Romania face off over an ethnic dispute," *Euractiv.com*, 21 February 2013, https://www.euractiv.com/section/languages-culture/opinion/hungary-and-romania-face-off-over-an-ethnic-dispute/ (accessed 30 Sept. 2016).

38. Zsolt Árus, "The Szeklers and their Struggle for Autonomy," Szekler National Council, 21 Nov. 2009, http://sznt.sic.hu/en/index.php?option=com_content&view=article&id=210:the-szeklers-and-their-struggle-for-autonomy&catid=4:a-szekelyseg&Itemid=6 (accessed 7 Sept. 2016).

39. The region called *Novorossiya* or New Russia was located in the western parts of Imperial Russia. It was invented in the late 18th century and has been used in the contemporary context as a historical image to invoke sentimental support for the aggression towards Ukraine by the post-Soviet Russian Federation since 2014. The project was shut down or suspended after the Minsk Agreement. Andrei Kolesnikov, "Why the Kremlin Is Shutting Down the Novorossiya Project," *Carnegie Endowment for International Peace*, 29 May 2015, http://carnegieendowment.org/2015/05/29/why-kremlin-is-shutting-down-novorossiya-project/i96u (accessed 7 Sept. 2016).

40. On schismogenesis, see Gregory Bateson, *Steps to an Ecology of Mind* (London: Jason Aronson Inc., 1987), 71–83.

Defending the Nation from her Nationalism(s)

JESENKO TEŠAN

This article offers and applies a framework for understanding nation-(re)-building after a major transition and crisis, like a war. It suggests socioanthropological concepts: liminality, mimesis, rites of passage, and tricksters. An understanding of the logic behind the emergence of nationalist tricksters can offer knowledge for an arguably better conflict-handling mechanism in deeply divided societies. It addresses, via the case study of Bosnia and Herzegovina (B&H), the following question: What is an adequate understanding of the postconflict self in B&H? The aim is to reconceptualize nationalism and the break-up of Yugoslavia (as well as the post-Dayton B&H) as a liminal process, in which trickster nationalists perpetuate schismatic conflict. The article concludes that trickster nationalists seem to be responsible for the current state of permanent liminality in B&H societies.

INTRODUCTION

In 1945, a certain form of nationalism, contaminated with fascism was dead, buried and gone. Nationalism perhaps, but not the nation. "Normally" an emerging nation looks like this: From the margins of a society, out of the ashes of a collapse, there arises a rock-solid single body. This single national body, due to her long sleep, when awakened at once can offer a priori knowledge of synthetic statements, as these reflect the conditions of possibility of a nation's conscious experience of things. It follows that a nation throws out — though already present in her — an embodiment of that fundamental national truth; namely, the nationalist who was carried in the nation's hands and rode the white horse, once he becomes an outsider to that same body, going against Your state that is not good for My nation.[1] Yet, in this century, nation (though worthy that name) and nationalism — which is her ideology — faces a new logic of war. Tricksters or quasi-nationalists who during the transitory moments of awakening, making use of liminal conditions and spinning imitative processes, through various techniques tinker with nationalism in order to gain the nation's imagination and consciousness. The social ideology of nation is under heavy attack. The question is not whether she can survive or not but rather what are the forces that are knocking on the nation's gates at this time in history?

To show these forces in vivo, the study explores two aspects of postcommunist and postconflict transition in Bosnia and Herzegovina (B&H) where the previous, tolerant (social) identity and habitus ("habitus" in the sense of Norbert Elias's term as nondiscursive practices and aspects of culture that bind people together) and identities are in a perpetual state of withering away, whilst artificial identities are assembled and injected into the body via political institutions, that is, the peace treaty structures. This article examines how living in "perpetual peace" becomes a mode of permanent liminality thus putting the nation(s) asleep. Yet, permanent liminality also applies to lasting war (violence), where the living self or the "I" is prevented from either living or dying. Here violence is understood as an intrinsic part of René Girard's concept of "mimetic desire" and "sacrificial mechanisms."[2] This attempt connects to Bateson's ideas concerning schismogenesis and the multiplication of error. Such a conceptual framework facilitates an understanding of the problematic character of a neither unification nor separation type situation, created by major postwar peace treaties like Versailles (after WWI) or Dayton (after the 1995 Bosnia and Herzegovina war).

Further, the article considers Immanuel Kant's idea on "Perpetual Peace" literally as "War Treaties." Instead of returning to a stable, ordinary situation the treaty institutions bounce the identity and the societies involved back into the realm of war, generating a paradoxical condition: perpetually "dividing society," forcing it to live in "permanent liminality." The self and identity are caught in a net of suspended roles associated both with communism and the mimetic violence of nationalism, where such (mis)identification through liminality becomes considered as normal and desirable. According to Szakolczai, permanent liminality is "the hypothetical situation where such a ritual becomes permanent; when individuals become stuck with their roles, which they must play from now onwards for the rest of their lives."[3] Explicitly, this article looks at the underlying genealogical processes that have enabled nation-building in Yugoslavia (within B&H), which was fundamentally not necessarily on weak foundations but rather on troubled, wild, and somewhat strange ones (see the Byzantine prehistory). I thus ask the following question: What is the *adequate* understanding of the postconflict self in B&H?

POLITICAL ANTHROPOLOGY: ETHNIC & RELIGIOUS MINORITIES

THE QUESTIONS POSED AND A CLARIFICATION

What is the root of the transgression of normality in the contemporary society of Bosnia and Herzegovina (B&H)? The day-to-day situation and practices (most notably architecture, cacophonic music, and dances) in this postconflict society signal social downfall and a losing of identity. The core societal situation in current B&H self and society could be labelled simply as an acute desire for moral nihilism. In this article, the term "self" is understood in terms of C. G. Jung's concept of self-centered self, rather than the ex-centric or schismatic self.[4] However, I opt not to use "subject," as this word has institutional and/or structuralist connotations. In particular, I locate the error-substances in a trickster attitude responsible for the U-turn process or deformation of the previous identity, thus forcing the self to flee into a newly constructed identity away from freedom, healing, and reality into conformity: nationalism, fascism, even inverted communism.

I argue that institutions, such as a peace treaty, can become disordered not because they are beyond any order, rather because they fixate a wrong attitude and identity at the wrong time and in the wrong way, institutionalizing mimetic modes of behavior in liminal moments, producing schismogenic identities as a pathological normalcy. In this way, it becomes easier to diagnose several error-substances. Firstly, the condition of institutionalized liminality allows the interactive forces of deconstruction and construction to operate in unison. In principle, once a treaty is signed and ratified, it becomes impossible to change it.[5] Secondly, the process of deconstructing the previous identity and assembling a new identity is assured via a specific instrument — postwar consociation — embedded in the signature of a political institution. Finally, the underlying forces behind the dividing society can be best analyzed by several anthropological concepts like "trickster," "liminality," "mimesis," and "schismogenesis." Thus, it follows that the root of the transgression of normality in a postconflict society and thus the failed democratization process lies in the condition of an institutionalized permanent liminality.[6]

However, when referring to nationalism and in particular to the question whether the — primordial — nation[7] precedes nationalism, the article argues that the nation follows nationalists, as nationalism is a reactive force to the policies of the modern state.[8] Thus, I cannot accept the completely romantic arguments for various reasons. My lived experience demonstrates the opposite is true. I was born in the Socialist Federative Republic of Yugoslavia in Bosnia and Herzegovina (B&H) Sarajevo, completed my elementary and high school education in the "Serbo-Croatian" language and held a Yugoslav passport. In this sense, my nation and nationalism was Yugoslavia(n). My surname is Orthodox while my forename is Belarus/Russian and means Autumn-Man. After 1995, I no longer could be Yugoslav nor could I speak Serbo-Croatian nor could I be Bosnian and Herzegovinian. So, I became American. This is why I accept in this context the constructivist argument: nationalism as an ideology that precedes the nation, which then in unison produce national identity and sentiments.[9] However, constructive argument in a sedentary (romantic) environment seems at the minimum problematic. The trickster and its nationalism of the 1990s led to an end to my identity and habitus. It crafts new nations, and, in turn, sedentary nationalism(s) interact with the Dayton Peace Agreement (DPA) in a deadly cocktail.

In addition, the nationality conflicts on the territory of the former Yugoslavia and, in particular, B&H are a par excellence example for the ideas of the modernist school of nationalism clashing with romantic attitudes. In that sense, I expand and apply John Breuilly's operative words "unification and separation"[10] for the 1990s in Yugoslavia. Thus, on the one hand, there was unification nationalism (see Germany and the European Union), while on the other separation nationalism, corresponding to the collapse of the socialist federations, the Union of Soviet Socialist Republics (USSR), Czechoslovakia, and Yugoslavia. In order to be able to revisit the meaning of how nationalism constructs and what is the substance that is responsible for the acute moral nihilism in current B&H society, we need to go further than the current, simplistic mantra about barbarism and the ancient hatreds in B&H and the Balkans.

The argument thus proceeds to indicate with a broad brush a specific Byzantine legacy, the undead spirits, which infiltrated the millet system of the Ottoman Empire (the "sick man of Europe"), and how these can in unison destroy a previous identity while fermenting nationalists' discourse thus de novo-nations (ethnoreligious groups). Ottoman imperial policies gave rise to nationalisms, which were reanimated and enshrined into the current postconflict consociational and federal mechanisms of postconflict constructed B&H. In that sense, the new identities in postconflict B&H live in institutionalized "permanent liminality."

RITES OF PASSAGE, SELF-FORMATION, AND LIMINALITY: BYZANTIUM, MILLETS, AND B&H

The theoretical framework of this study is provided by the term liminality. Liminality is the processual and experiential ground in which the action of individuals can be understood in a broader network of collective processes. The word "liminality" originates from the Latin word "limen," something situated in between. The etymological root of this term possesses precise anthropological meaning.[11] Liminality means that something or someone is in suspension or at a threshold, or a midpoint between a beginning and an end. The term was developed by Arnold van Gennep and later

Victor Turner in their studies of rites of passage.[12] For example, the suspension — limen — might manifest itself as an arrested process of transformation, in the analogy of a rite of passage, in which the past never ends and so the future can never begin. The condition is a proto-present, explicated in Szakolczai's term "permanent liminality." The site of an arrested rite of passage or "permanent liminality" is dangerous. In short, the research traces the *gestures* of the "masters" who during the liminal moments entrap human imagination and institutions into a treacherous, permanent spiraling liminality, and who are thus identified as *tricksters*, including some *contemporary politicians* who target individuals and groups in order to appease popular concerns.

Moreover, rites of passage, part of liminality, such as the rites around birth, the move to adulthood, marriage, or death, are central for identity formation. They mark the transition from one stage of life to the next but without the cut/schism. They offer something new for a person or group, that is, an element of "individuation" or a seamless feeling of membership in a community.[13] The rites have three stages, under the one umbrella of liminality: separation, performance, and aggregation. During the rite, the whole order of society is suspended, until those who participate in the rite (initiands) gain a new "identity" under the supervision of the "Master" of the ceremony.[14] As Victor Turner explains, the ritual is a "living ritual" above all. He says: "Ritual is, in its most typical cross-cultural expression, a synchronization of many performative genres, and is often ordered by dramatic structure. [...] All the senses of participants and performers may be engaged; they hear music and prayers, see visual symbols, taste consecrated foods, smell incense, and touch sacred persons and objects."[15]

A rite of passage (as a living ritual) thus enables, with the help of a Master of Ceremonies, to preserve and perpetuate imagination, thus habitus, manners, and society. Therefore, the character and quality of the master is crucial to the outcome. If the master is mimed or a trickster, the rite often stalls in "permanent liminality," becoming a living nightmare in which spirits of the undead inhabit the void of destruction. Such a permanent liminality creates an extraordinarily dangerous situation for society and individuals, which Gregory Bateson frames as "schismogenesis."[16] Thus, as much as the rite in itself is demanding, so is the role of the master in conducting the rite and trying to stave off the trickster. However, when trickster replaces the true master and when individuals and societies start on troubled foundations, the transition mutates within this void. In other words, "Bateson's rule" and schismogenesis become normalcy regardless of cultural milieu.

This article thus uses liminality as a tool to understand the context of the Byzantine Empire, in itself liminal, in order to extract the certain spin or "Spirit" responsible for the hijacking, inversion, and parody of imagination. The analysis accentuates and examines the negative side of the

Byzantine legacy, which Ahrweiler perhaps might include in her category of "barbarian," and which is called "Spirit" by Szakolczai. In Helene Ahrweiler's terminology, the virtuous habitus of the Byzantine "spirit" focuses on the uplifting and freeing legacy of humanism, virtue, and broadmindedness.[17] However, this research expands on Ahrweiler's lower term "barbarian" and tries to capture it as the spirit that employs sophistry and trickery in order to constrain and limit human potential and freedom via liminality.

TRICKSTER IDENTITY (DE)FORMATION UNDER PERMANENT SPLITTING AND LIMINALITY

During liminal transitory moments and especially after the peace agreement has been signed and ratified, the old "habitus" and identity enters a final deformation. Norbert Elias develops the concept "habitus" in the *Civilizing Process* in order to show how a given social structure, like the royal court, dictates and/or encompasses habits and patterns of behavior of particular people, leading towards common understanding or encapsulation into a "civilizing process."[18] In the light of Plato's response to decaying Athenian democracy, closely following Wydra's argument on democratic experience, though applied onto the case study of B&H, after the DPA the social-habitus[19] prior to the war was replaced by a code-of-conduct rooted in a collectivized ethno-cum-religious responsibility, suggested by the legacy of trickster figures. This process can be called a quasi-unifying nationalism that is following trickster gestures.

For instance, the social-habitus in B&H prior to the conflict was a kind of odd identity. It confused many internationals (outsiders). Bosnians could not understand why internationals keep insisting on a "clear-cut" definition of ethnicity and/or nationality. Bosnian and Herzegovinian men and women when asked the question "What is your nationality?" would automatically shiver. For every Bosnian and Herzegovinian that question, prior to the 1992 war, was the highest possible insult one could inflict. Almost automatically the community would cut off that person from any social participation. Indeed, this unspoken pattern of social-identity, though not necessarily civic as in France and/or the United States, may explain why the new elites' firing discourses, Šešelj along with Izetbegović and Tudjman in the 1970s and most recently Karadjić in the 1990s, turned against this naturally odd habitus.

To help understand the social change and/or identity deformation, in the nondiscursive gestures or patterns that bind people together, several anthropological concepts are needed. Trickster, in particular, is a useful concept, as it captures what is diabolic, schismatic, infectious, and above all is a mask in itself.[20] Under difficult transitory moments, a trickster or a "mask," following on and expanding Pizzorno's argument, infects individuals and society, while constructing changes in identity. The schism and scission, as studied by Bateson is extremely important for this case study. It shows that once schism has been institutionalized and with the help of tricksters a schismogenic reason can be created, thus fostering a schismatic and ex-centric identity. In that sense, due to the schism or cut the internal violence spins from within individuals, and society is never able to reach a resolution.[21] Voegelin argues that Gnosticism is the consequence of an internal schism, resulting in a gnostic revolt. In that sense, the tricksters' legacy can become embodied in nationalism. It then goes on to promote a schism of the previous "habitus" via mimetic violence and generating a pathological condition, as the concept of "we," or a community of dependence, rather than the "whole individual" or a (civic) self with integrity. The schism is indispensable for modern dictatorships.[22]

However, the point is not to contest the "imagined" nation idea or civic nations; rather, what is meant here is that it is the trickster nationalist, rather than capitalism and/or the print culture, who may hold sway in "spontaneous" remapping and rearranging the mental furniture of the nation-imagination in order to transpose it into virulent nationalism. In this pathological condition, open schism and blindness, implying a permanently promoted liminality, seem to lie the success of modern tricksters, "technology," and even the modernist interpretation on nationalism.[23] Such "spontaneous ethical impulses," according to Jung are fundamental for the individuation, and are fundamentally different from the Kantian notion of "transcendental deduction."

In particular, in Kant's terminology the self-deduction is expressed that "I have no *knowledge* of myself as I am but merely as I appear to myself [...] I exist as an intelligence which is conscious solely of its power of combination [...] The 'I think' expresses the act of determining my existence."[24] It follows that, in this case study, an *almost* spontaneous — self-realized — I appeared (though different from Kant's egocentric one who is awaiting the "leader"), but it was arrested into the liminal problem. In other words, Jung's "individuation" process and Adrian Guelke's "politics of imitation" highlight the problems of both the "imagined" nation idea and its "applicability" or uploading it into the healthy democracy immune to tricksters. In that sense, I argue that when such a priori imagined idea is hijacked by a trickster-leader; during the liminal moments, it becomes easier to understand how the civic idea on nation may not work. In particular, how it is possible that a temporary situation of transition could become a lasting, suspended condition. Thence, what is the root of the transgression of normality into pathological state in the contemporary society of B&H seems to lie in what I define as a U-turn related to perpetual peace treaties as war treaties. These in union seem to perpetuate a permanent schism at the individual and social levels thus preserving the tricksters' logic.[25]

It would be no exaggeration, following Guelke's line of thought, to argue that in ethnically divided societies dictatorship can continue to exist outside communism, in spite of accepting formally the principles of democracy, precisely as dictatorship depends on mimesis and egocentric and schismatic selfhood.[26] Then a political anthropology of transformative experiences, through awareness about trickster figures, and theories of the imitative self, including the mentality of the crowd, leads to the core question of this article: *What is the adequate understanding of the self in postconflict settings?*

A question similar to mine was posed by Erik Ringmar: "What [...] is the proper understanding of the self in modern society?"[27] At first, it seems that these two questions are fundamentally different, and not related to each other. However, they are very much about the same topic: the formation of the modern (civic) self and especially its imagination, something fundamental to understanding political processes. Note that the emphasis is on an *adequate* understanding of the self, because I wish to acknowledge the success of some peace treaties and democratic transitions but highlight that the consolidation of success (civic self) cannot occur in the absence of a deliberate self (individuated self).

OTTOMAN MILLETS AND GESTURES OF NATIONALISM

In referring to Byzantium, one inevitably must face the situation that "[f]or the English-speaking world of the twenty-first century, or the world of western Europe in general, Byzantium is something of a black hole, a shadowy force if known at all, unlike the empire of West Rome whose physical remains are conspicuous and very real reminders of its former presence."[28] That "black hole" and "shadowy force" suggest the liminal nature of Byzantine. Yet, this "dark" or "nil" spirit, to borrow from Horvath's terminology, appears multifaceted rather than singular, hence hard to capture. This mutating spirit presents an alienated and excessive pathos, which in the Ottoman Empire led to a "politics of extremes" or the "sick man of Europe."

The label "sick man of Europe" also relates to a fundamental question posed by Szakolczai: "whether there was any philosophy [philosophers] in the Byzantine world."[29] The implication is that sophistry and tricksters rather than philosophers and real masters provided leadership in the political and social realms. Accordingly, from a sociological perspective the Ottoman Empire was the direct successor of the Byzantine spirit, characterized by a replacement of philosophy with sophistry and tragedy with comedy.

POLITICAL ANTHROPOLOGY: ETHNIC & RELIGIOUS MINORITIES

A CASE STUDY OF THE MILLET SYSTEM AS FORMING PROTO-NATIONS' NATIONALISM(S)

The Ottomans' millets were political and geographical enclaves, based on ethnoreligious differences inherited from Byzantium and intended to separate populations and religions. Ivo Banac succinctly explains this "accommodative" process of the millet system in relation to the eastern Mediterranean, in particular, the creation of Serbian national character. It is worth quoting in full:

> This was an aspect of the so-called *millet* system, whereby the non-Muslim subjects of the Porte were provided with an autonomous self-government under their respective religious leaders, the term conveying both nationality and religion in the Ottoman scheme of things. The non-Muslim *millets* (Orthodox, Jewish, Armenian) were subject to their own native regulations and to the Şeriat (Islamic Law). Their dealings with the Ottoman state were conducted through their respective community leaders. As ethnarchs of the Serbs, the patriarch of Peć thus had not only all the prerogatives of their spiritual station but also the authority that belonged to the medieval Serbian kings.[30]

In addition, this system of "autonomy" offered to different religious groups gave certain commercial privileges to European merchants and their ideas. The millet system thus enabled the infiltration of western ideas, particularly the civic French torch of "liberty," deep into the Ottoman Empire. Furthermore, the system's policy of juggling populations became critical in light of external threats. The question is whether the millets at the end of the 19th and the beginning of the 20th centuries turned out to be proto-nations, rather than just religious communities.[31] Halil Inalcik contends that the millets of "Non-Muslim communities under the Ottomans" could, under Islamic law, *convert* to the "True Religion" or remain second-class "citizens." The non-Muslim population would be "voluntarily" imagining and assimilated into Islam, as in the case of the Balkans.[32] In other words, for Inalcik the problem of "minority" and different religious groups was solved by separation and noncontact.

Moreover, in *The Birth of the Modern World 1780–1914*, C. A. Bayly enquires into the identity of the empire and its people. According to Bayly, the Sultan was at the same time "Ottoman Khan, a Caesar [...] and later Khalifa, or successor, to the Prophet and a universal king in the style of Alexander." The Sultan was a Muslim ruler and his regime could only provide "patronage" for different religious groups through the millet systems.[33] The Ottoman Empire differed from within, due to an exceptional element, namely, a different "world-view," Islam, as to who are the chosen people, how it practices patronage, and how it accommodates groups. The position of the Sultan and the population policies illustrate the continuous legacy of the Byzantine Empire. The undead spirit of Byzantium infested the Ottoman Empire, festering the disease of the sick man. Thus, regarding the Eastern Question, the Ottoman Empire's "tolerant" policies and above all the treatment of the conquered territory and the population were "different" from western colonial policies but not necessarily better.

Indeed, Itzkowitz argues that if non-Muslims (gnostic sects like Bogomils, Orthodox Serbs, Catholics, and Jews) in millets did not convert to Islam, their social and political status would not be lifted beyond that of second-class citizens.[34] Todorova claims that the "Ottoman Legacy" continued deep into popular culture in the Balkans. Its "legacy" was indeed "inhibiting" imagination, but Todorova seems to dislocate such inhibiting force from "spirit" and imagination into "traditions" and "continuity."[35] Such inhibiting processes helped the legacy of the sick man of Europe to "survive" via "particular attitudes." The millet was an "accommodative" modern method of dividing and policing religious groups by giving, indirectly, enough room for indigenous national ideology to fester within the Ottoman Empire, provided that it did not clash with Islam as the core-ethnos religion. It is debatable as to what extent this "power-sharing" and "accommodative" mechanism was similar to the early modern European nation-state formation.[36]

In order to appease the "internal" threats, millets thus offered, especially after the Tanzimat "perestroika,"[37] an engine for the construction of proto-civic nation-states via strategies of primitive power-sharing, partition, secession, and federalism. Thus, through division and the forceful conversion or naturalization (both linguistic and religious) of locals into a new religion (Islam), the millets proved the best method to construct and strengthen the empire, thus the legacy, a most durable political mechanism for dividing and ruling, but, also and more importantly, it had begun to awaken the sleeping beauty from sleep as a response to the imperial "objective" policies.

POSTCOMMUNIST AND POSTCONFLICT DEMOCRATIZATION AND THE IMMOLATED B&H SELF

In the course of Eastern European unification and separation, expanding on Breuilly's argument, new (civic) constructed nationalisms presented difficult challenges to selfhood. In my opinion and from an institutionalist aspect, however, while to some extent I concur with Sumantra Bose, I partly must disagree. Bose argues that "the Bosnian state is not about to wither away, if only because its inherent weakness is compensated in part by the resolve of the 'international community' that a Bosnian state should survive, and the protracted effort invested by the 'community' of powerful states, regional

European institutions and multilateral organizations to ensure that survival."[38] The overwhelming evidence from the ground shows that the modern state may survive but the society, or for the purposes of this argument the nation, is likely to fall into liminal sleep again rather than collapse. Thus, Bose is only partly correct in his analysis.

What I am particularly interested in is to demonstrate Adrian Guelke's argument and to expand my view that constructed democracy in the East is a failure. The project does not work everywhere due to the dividing forces (romantic versus civic) of nationalisms, which then go on to divide society.[39] Unlike Guelke, however, I would like to propose that the postconflict selfhood in B&H is indeed divided. It creates new schismatic identity. This duality of a divided and heterogeneous but also postconflict setting constitutes a complex problem and very sick democratic state, which can be fully grasped via the state of permanent liminality.

In that sense, B&H's identity is in a permanent cut or schism. It is not liberated, healed and transformed into a centered/complete identity. The result is that Guelke is correct that division is desired, but this desire seems to lie in the war/violence-related fear of homeostasis thence democracy. In that sense, it is obvious that the process of individuation or self-realization cannot happen, as it is exposed to the schismatic forces of unification and separation.

Indeed, one can observe that there are some anomalies in the formation of self and society during the liminal multiple transitions. For instance, if a given context, postcommunist and postconflict environment, does not present an obstacle, then there ought to be some sort of normalization towards self-realization. Indeed, this happens in B&H and other postconflict environments, but in verso. The self is in a cut between an ex-centric and centric self. As Jung argues:

> The ego stands to the self as the moved to the mover, or as object to subject, because the determining factors which radiate out from the self surround the ego on all sides and are therefore supraordinate to it. The self, like the unconscious, is an *a priori* existent out of which the ego evolves. It is, so to speak, an unconscious prefiguration of the ego. It is not I who create myself, rather I happen to myself.[40]

Thus, unlike Kantian transcendentalism, Jungian philosophy does not transcend or destroy the self. According to Jung, it is integrating the ego and the unconscious *ad infinitum*. Yet, in the context of this article — a legacy of undead spirits — B&H's liminal multiple transitions had left her identity in a state of the immolated-self, thus the ego is under pressure towards negating or transcending itself. The ego is enriched by the schismatic forces, which feed into a spiraling and mimetic egocentrism: hypercivic identity. The tensions towards separation and cutting produce egocentrics who further assemble quasi-nation-nationalism attitudes. The Jungian process in de novo B&H is impossible.

CONFLICT HANDLING

Where there are people, there inevitably will be conflict. Conflict is not an unnatural event. It emerges as a natural product of different expectations, differences in opinions, disagreements, and so on. However, the problem arises when conflict turns into a permanent state, as in post-Dayton B&H society. The analysis has shown that forces of unification and separation ferment conflict. In particular, this situation leads towards extreme forms of marginal or fringe-nationalisms, which are considered as a part of vague impulses that have not yet been awakened into a full political force. This is clearly vivid in the context of the egocentric societies arising out of post-nationality conflicts behind the peaceful "lines" in "the Troubled" regions: Bosnia (Sarajevo/Mostar), Northern Ireland (Belfast), and Lebanon (Beirut). The management and resolution of violent ethnic conflicts, as Guelke argues, is vital for the global community.[41]

Under the influence of tricksters, these schismatic impulses can quickly become a mass habitus, encapsulated by institutions as a concrete political formation for *not* resolving the root of ethnic conflict. Guelke is right that "the adoption of dictatorial policies by the democratically elected government" may lead to a failure of democracy.[42] He furthermore emphasizes the lacuna in the global mantra of international relations and political science experts that political accommodation in divided societies depends on specific conflict-management instruments, such as consociationalism and/or asymmetric federalism, which would lead to peace and a type of civic democracy. This scenario fails to capture what happens on the ground in postconflict environments. Or, in Guelke's words: "consociationalism's emphasis on the management of divisions over the *healing* [emphasis added] of divisions runs counter to efforts to transcend divisions at a grass-roots level that characterises the civil society approach."[43] Thus, a political accommodation that starts from the premises of "the management of divisions" after the peace agreement presents a par excellence example of nonhealing-and-nonaccommodative instruments for conflict resolution. This is why I define such a peace treaty as a war treaty.

It follows that to be a whole again, or personally liberated and healed from grotesque violence, the "political accommodation" must start from the premise of the concrete human being. Conflict management is based on a Kantian philosophy of transcendence, that is, overcoming or negating the unconscious. This process, "transcendental idealism," or cutting different interpretations of a given object ad infinitum goes against Jung's arguments on unifying (appropriating) ego and self into one self-centered individual. Individuation, closely following Jung, is thus a permanent active self-formation for handling conflicts towards not just tolerance but unifying rather separating — cutting — differences of opinion and disagreements within an a priori identity. As Jung states:

> Conscious and unconscious do not make a whole when one of them is suppressed and injured by the other. If they must contend, let it at least be a fair fight with equal rights on both sides. Both are aspects of life. Consciousness should defend its reason and protect itself, and the chaotic life of the unconscious should be given the chance of having its way too — as much of it as we can stand. This means open conflict and open collaboration at once. That, evidently, is the way human life should be. It is the old game of hammer and anvil: between them the patient iron is forged into an indestructible whole, an "individual." This, roughly, is what I mean by the individuation process.[44]

The DPA as introduced as an artificial vaccination and new habitus for a romantic society where the schismatic forces of two nationalisms — unifying and separating — formed a hypnotic state. This spinning wheel of permanent liminality confirms Turner's idea that in liminality anything is possible; hence, ethnic cleansing was a direct manifestation of the desire for mimetic violence and sacrifice. The B&H case study represents a crisis in democracy on a global scale and is a model case for the mistaken technology of conflict resolution that systematically eliminates those elements of the previous habitus that could lead society out of the deconstructive, sophist/trickster "particular attitude" back towards a unified self.

CONCLUSION

This article has discussed the challenges postconflict and postcommunist societies face after a peace treaty has been signed, determining the neither-here-nor-there condition in light of this case study, the former Yugoslav society within B&H. This article has shown that nationalism was not the only factor that contributed to the staled transition, a condition of institutionalized liminality. Thus, the "cut" that happened in the society sometime in mid-1993 was not only due to the nationalisms. However, it seems it did contribute to a paradoxical liminal moment that involved in unison pathogenesis and schismogenesis. Society made a sudden U-turn: Instead of unification, it opted for separation, due to nationalist tricksters. Self and society were arrested and infected again by the legacy of the "undead" spirit. Therefore, this article placed overall emphasis on the better understanding on when (timing) is nation rather than what (history, name, territory, or symbolism) is nation.

Finally, going back to Max Weber who introduced the three ideal types of legitimate authority—charismatic, traditional, and legal—it should be mentioned that these need to be "adjusted," to tap into Guelke's vocabulary, by Horvath's study on trickster. Weber warned already in January of 1919, in the midst of the Versailles Treaty negotiations that "[n]ot summer's bloom lies ahead of us, but rather a polar night of icy darkness and hardness."[45] In that sense, the icy nights seem, in my view, to represent a transitory moment, metamorphosing charisma and trickster into one hybrid: trickster nationalist, that is, quasi-nationalist as a result of the stolen transition, a condition that invites the institutionalization of permanent liminality. Agnes Horvath's extensive study on trickster logic and its malleability thus complements Weber's idea of charisma with the trickster, particularly relevant concerning nationalism. However, to elaborate on the specifics of the Horvath/Weber axis and the trickster nationalists' gestures is beyond the scope of this article. Its aim was rather modest in highlighting two forces, separation and unification: separating from communism and "creating" a unified polity but betrayed by the tricksters who then hijacked the nation and the transition. Trickster nationalists abused and utilized nationalism(s) as a technology to produce a U-turn or an open cut into the nation, from which undead spirits fester.

ACKNOWLEDGMENTS

This article is part of a larger PhD study. Parts of Chapter 2 have been presented by Joan Davison and Jesenko Tešan on 21–27 Aug. 2016 at the 23rd International Congress of Byzantine Studies in Belgrade, Serbia.

NOTES

1. This closely follows John Breuilly's argument on nationalism; see John Breuilly, *Nationalism and the State* (Manchester: Manchester University Press, 2001).
2. René Girard was not the only one who emphasized mimesis in human behavior. Before him, it was Gabriel Tarde as a founder of imitation in sociology and above all Plato. In this analysis, Girard is important in the sense that his concepts help highlight the production and dissemination of violent mimetic human behavior; see René Girard, *Deceit, Desire, and the Novel: Self and Other in Literary Structure* (Baltimore: Johns Hopkins University Press, 1976); René Girard, *The Scapegoat* (London: Athlone, 1986); René Girard, *"To Double Business Bound": Essays on Literature, Mimesis, and Anthropology* (London: Athlone Press, 1988); and René Girard, *Violence and the Sacred* (London: Continuum, 2005). Whilst adding the role of trickster, it becomes clearer how confusion is generated and responsible for pathogenesis, schismogenesis, and U-turn processes.
3. Arpad Szakolczai, *Reflexive Historical Sociology* (London: Routledge, 2000), 213.
4. Carl Gustav Jung, *The Undiscovered Self* (London: Routledge, 1958).
5. Agreeing that the treaty really was supposed to be a perpetual peace treaty; however, the analysis due to the practical constraints cannot follow an in-depth study on either Kant's notion on it or the key ingredients, discourses, and/or consequences of the Dayton agreement. For such an analysis, the author points the readership to his PhD thesis, Jesenko Tešan, "Perpetual Peace Treaty as War: A Study in Permanent Liminality" (University College Cork), which in detail unpacks the key elements on the

substantiation of trickster nationalists' logic (for example, some discourses or quotes taken from Milosevic, Izetbegovic, or Karadzic, and above all 1992 war archives from Sarajevo). Therein lie the crucial evidences of failed democratization due to the structural and trickster nationalists' engineered condition of failed democratization with the help of war and grotesque human rights abuses in B&H, what the author defines as a U-turn (inverted communism) process.

6. Due to the practical constraints, the example from my larger research (Tešan, "Perpetual Peace Treaty as War: A Study in Permanent Liminality") can only be mentioned at this moment, the flag, the bridge in Mostar, and Dayton Peace Agreement (DPA) in B&H appear to represent "allness" and "connect" attitudes. The flag represents all and recognizes nationalisms. The DPA clearly gestures and represents all while its consociationalism mechanism is responsive to nationalisms. Along with federalism, it is a response to nationalism and ethno-cum-religious conflict, being an attempt to solve it, but it fails. The constructed, fake bridge in Mostar gestures in attempting to "connect" and, thus, overcoming the wounds of wars. Yet, because it is externally imposed, it fails to overcome the nationalisms, precisely because it is artificial (see Tešan, "Perpetual Peace Treaty as War: A Study in Permanent Liminality").

7. Adrian Hastings, *The Construction of Nationhood: Ethnicity, Religion and Nationalism* (Cambridge: Cambridge University Press, 1997); Theodor Schieder, *Nationalismus und Nationalstaat: Studien zum nationalen Problem im modernen Europa* (Göttingen: Vandenhoeck & Ruprecht, 1992); Hans-Ulrich Wehler, *Nationalismus: Geschichte, Formen, Folgen* (Munich: C. H. Beck, 2001).

8. Breuilly, *Nationalism and the State*; E. J. Hobsbawm, *Nations and Nationalism since 1780: Programme, Myth, Reality* (Cambridge: Cambridge University Press, 1990).

9. For similar arguments, see Elie Kedourie, *Politics in the Middle East* (Oxford: Oxford University Press, 1992); Elie Kedourie, *Nationalism* (Oxford: Blackwell, 1993).

10. Breuilly, *Nationalism and the State*, 123–154 (on separate nationalism); 340–362 (on unification).

11. Agnes Horvath, "The Genealogy of Political Alchemy: The Technological Invention of Identity Change," in Agnes Horvath, Bjørn Thomassen, and Harald Wydra, eds., *Breaking Boundaries: Varieties of Liminality* (New York: Berghahn Books, 2015), 72–92; Bjørn Thomassen, "Notes Towards an Anthropology of Political Revolutions," *Comparative Studies in Society and History* 54(3): 679–706 (2012); Bjørn Thomassen, "Thinking with Liminality: to the Boundaries of an Anthropological Concept," in Agnes Horvath, Bjørn Thomassen, and Harald Wydra, eds., *Breaking Boundaries: Varieties of Liminality* (New York: Berghahn Books, 2015), 39–58; Harald Wydra, *Communism and the Emergence of Democracy* (Cambridge: Cambridge University Press, 2007); Harald Wydra, "Liminality and Democracy," in Agnes Horvath, Bjørn Thomassen, and Harald Wydra, eds., *Breaking Boundaries: Varieties of Liminality* (New York: Berghahn Books, 2015), 183–204; Harald Wydra, "The Liminal Origins of Democracy," *International Political Anthropology* 2(1): 91–109 (2009).

12. Arnold van Gennep, *The Rites of Passage* (Chicago: University of Chicago Press, 1960); Victor Turner, *The Forest of Symbols: Aspects of the Ndembu Ritual* (Ithaca, NY: Cornell University Press, 1967); Victor Turner, *The Ritual Process: Structure and Anti-Structure* (New York: De Gruyter, 1969); in addition see other works by Victor Turner, *Blazing the Trail: Waymarks in the Exploration of Symbols* (Tucson: University of Arizona Press, 1992); Victor Turner, *From Ritual to Theatre: The Human Seriousness of Play* (New York: Performing Arts Journal Publications, 1982).

13. Arpad Szakolczai, *Comedy and the Public Sphere: The Re-Birth of Theatre as Comedy and the Genealogy of the Modern Public Arena* (London: Routledge, 2013); Arpad Szakolczai, "Dreams, Visions and Utopias: Romantic and Realist Revolutionaries, and the Idyllic," in M. H. Jacobsen and K. Tester, eds., *Utopia: Social Theory and the Future* (Farnham, Surrey: Ashgate, 2012), 47–68; Arpad Szakolczai, "Identity Formation Mechanisms: A Conceptual and Genealogical Analysis," *EUI Working Paper* SPS No. 98/2: 1–43 (1998); Arpad Szakolczai, "Liminality and Experience: Structuring Transitory Situations and Transformative Events," in Agnes Horvath, Bjørn Thomassen, and Harald Wydra, eds., *Breaking Boundaries: Varieties of Liminality* (New York: Berghahn Books, 2015), 11–38; Arpad Szakolczai, *Permanent Liminality and Modernity* (London: Routledge, 2016); Arpad Szakolczai, *Reflexive Historical Sociology* (London: Routledge, 2000); Arpad Szakolczai, *The Genesis of Modernity* (London: Routledge, 2003).

14. Turner, *The Ritual Process*, 94–95.

15. Turner, *From Ritual to Theatre*, 81–84.

16. Gregory Bateson, *Naven* (Stanford, CA: Stanford University Press, 1958).

17. Hélène Ahrweiler, *The Making of Europe: Lectures and Studies* (Athens: Nea Synora, 2000), 46–47, 68–69, 79, and, in particular, 116.

18. See Norbert Elias, *The Civilizing Process: The History of Manners and State Formation and Civilization* (Oxford: Blackwell, 1994); Norbert Elias, *The Court Society* (Oxford: Blackwell, 1983); Norbert, Elias, *The Society of Individuals* (Dublin: University College Dublin Press, 2010).

19. On a similar argument, I closely follow Harald Wydra. He argues that the notion of "civic culture," or as he says, "Democratic civility, therefore, was not predetermined by a model of democracy coming from 'outside,' but has to be reconstructed from within the communist experience"; see Harald Wydra, "Democratisation as Meaning-Formation – Lessons from the Communist Experience," *International Political Anthropology* 1(1): 113–32 (2008); see also Wydra, "The Liminal Origins of Democracy," 96–97.

20. Agnes Horvath and Bjørn Thomassen, "Mimetic Errors in Liminal Schismogenesis: On the Political Anthropology of the Trickster," *International Political Anthropology* 1(1): 3–24 (2008); Agnes Horvath, "Liminality and the Unreal Class of the Image-Making Craft," *International Political Anthropology* 2(1): 53–72 (2009); Agnes Horvath, "Mythology and the Trickster," in Alexander Wöll and Harald Wydra, eds., *Democracy and Myth in Russia and Eastern Europe* (London: Routledge, 2008), 27–45; Agnes Horvath, "Pulcinella, or the Metaphysics of the Nulla: In Between Politics and Theatre," *History of the Human Sciences* 23(2): 46–67 (2010); Agnes Horvath, "Regression into Technology, or the First Mask," *International Political Anthropology* 3(2): 203–216 (2010); Horvath, "The Genealogy of Political Alchemy," 72–92; Agnes Horvath, "The Trickster Motive in Renaissance Political Thought," *Philosophia* (52): 95–111 (2007); Agnes Horvath, "Tricking into the Position of the Outcast: A Case Study in the Emergence and Effects of Communist Power," *Political Psychology* 19(2): 331–47 (1998); Alessandro Pizzorno, "The Mask: An Essay," *International Political Anthropology* 3(1): 5–28 (2010).

21. Carl Gustav Jung, *The Collected Works, Vol. 9, A Study in the Process of Individuation* (London: Routledge, 1964), 267; Carl Gustav Jung, *The Collected Works, Vol. 10, Civilization in Transition* (London: Routledge, 1964), 252–77.

22. Adrian Guelke, *Democracy and Ethnic Conflict: Advancing Peace in Deeply Divided Societies* (Basingstoke, New York: Palgrave Macmillan, 2004); Adrian Guelke, *Politics in Deeply Divided Societies* (Cambridge: Polity, 2012).

23. Benedict Anderson, *Imagined Communities: Reflections on the Origin and Spread of Nationalism* (London: Verso, 1983); Ernest Gellner, *Nationalism* (London: Weidenfeld & Nicolson, 1997); Ernest Gellner, *Nations and Nationalism* (Oxford: Basil Blackwell, 1983).

24. Immanuel Kant, *Critique of Pure Reason* (New York: St. Martin's Press, 1965), 158–59.

25. Guelke, *Democracy and Ethnic Conflict*, 181–82.

26. Ibid., 242.

27. Erik Ringmar, "The Problem of the Modern Self: Imitation, Will Power and the Politics of Character," *International Political Anthropology* 9(1): 67–86 (2016).

28. Elizabeth Jeffreys, John F. Haldon, and Robin Cormack, "Byzantine Studies as an Academic Discipline," in Elizabeth Jeffreys, John F. Haldon, and Robin Cormack, eds., *The Oxford Handbook of Byzantine Studies* (Oxford: Oxford University Press, 2008), 3–20, especially 4.

29. Szakolczai, *Comedy*, 120.

30. Ivo Banac, "Nationalism in Serbia," in Günay Göksu Özdoğan and Kemâli Saybaşılı, eds., *Balkans: A Mirror of the New International Order* (Istanbul: Eren, 1995), 134–52; see also Ivo Banac, *The National Question in Yugoslavia: Origins, History, Politics* (Ithaca, NY: Cornell University Press, 1984).

31. William L. Cleveland and Martin Bunton, *A History of the Modern Middle East* (Oxford: Westview Press, 2009), 157–61, 163, 168, 207, 231.

32. Halil Inalcik, "The Meaning of Legacy: The Ottoman Case," in L. Carl Brown, ed., *Imperial Legacy: The Ottoman Imprint on the Balkans and the Middle East* (New York: Columbia University Press, 1996), 23–24; *The Ottoman Empire: The Classical Age 1300–1600* (New Rochelle, NY: Aristide D. Caratzas, 1973); see also K. K. Barbir, "Memory, Heritage, and History: The Ottomans and the Arabs," in L. Carl Brown, ed., *Imperial Legacy: The Ottoman Imprint on the Balkans and the Middle East* (New York: Columbia University Press, 1996), 100–114.

33. C. A. Bayly, *The Birth of the Modern World, 1780–1914: Global Connections and Comparisons* (Oxford: Blackwell, 2004), 34, 59.

34. N. Itzkowitz, "The Problem of Perceptions," in L. Carl Brown, ed., *Imperial Legacy: The Ottoman Imprint on the Balkans and the Middle East* (New York: Columbia University Press, 1996), 30–38.

35. Mariia N. Todorova, "The Ottoman Legacy in the Balkans," in Günay Göksu Özdoğan and Kemâli Saybaşılı, eds., *Balkans: A Mirror of the New International Order* (Istanbul: Eren, 1995), 55–74; Mariia N. Todorova, *Imagining the Balkans* (New York: Oxford University Press, 1997); see also, Mariia

N. Todorova, "The Ottoman Legacy in the Balkans," in L. Carl Brown, ed., *Imperial Legacy: The Ottoman Imprint on the Balkans and the Middle East* (New York: Columbia University Press, 1996), 45–77; see also P. Salem, *The Bitter Legacy: Ideology and Politics in the Arab World* (New York: Cambridge University Press, 2009).

36. Brubaker Rogers, *Citizenship and Nationhood in France and Germany* (Cambridge, MA: Harvard University Press, 1994); see also Elie Kedourie, *Politics in the Middle East* (Oxford: Oxford University Press, 1992).

37. Roderic H. Davison, *Reform in the Ottoman Empire, 1856–1876* (Princeton: Princeton University Press, 1963).

38. Bose Sumantra, "The Bosnian State a Decade after Dayton," *International Peacekeeping* 12(3): 322–35 (2005); see also Bose Sumantra, *Bosnia after Dayton: Nationalist Partition and International Intervention* (London: Hurst, 2002); Bose Sumantra, *Contested Lands: Israel-Palestine, Kashmir, Bosnia, Cyprus, and Sri Lanka* (Cambridge, MA: Harvard University Press, 2007); Bose Sumantra, *States, Nations, Sovereignty: Sri Lanka, India, and the Tamil Eelam Movement* (Thousand Oaks, CA: Sage, 1994).

39. Adrian Guelke, *Politics in Deeply Divided Societies* (Cambridge: Polity, 2012).

40. Carl Gustav Jung, *The Collected Works, Vol. 11, Psychology and Religion: West and East* (London: Routledge, 1958), 391.

41. Adrian Guelke, *Democracy and Ethnic Conflict: Advancing Peace in Deeply Divided Societies* (Basingstoke: Palgrave, 2004), 239.

42. Ibid., 242.

43. Ibid., 243.

44. Carl Gustav Jung, *The Collected Works, Vol. 7, A Study in The Process of Individuation* (London: Routledge, 1954), 288.

45. Max Weber, "Politics as a Vocation," in H. H. Gerth and C. Wright Mills, eds., *From Max Weber: Essays in Sociology* (London: Routledge, 1948), 12.

Reconciliation and After in Northern Ireland: The Search for a Political Order in an Ethnically Divided Society

DUNCAN MORROW

Since Westphalia, territoriality has been a critical element in the political management of violence. Where legitimacy was contested, as in the area that became Northern Ireland, territorial disputes often escalated into significant violence. The importance to human futures of controlling violence is the central theme of the work of Rene Girard. This article explores the implications of Girardian thinking for understanding both the escalation of violence in Northern Ireland after the 1960s and efforts to escape the dictates of territoriality in the peace that followed. In particular, it explores the concept of reconciliation and its application amidst endemic political rivalry.

TERRITORY, LEGITIMACY, AND VIOLENCE AFTER EMPIRE

Since 1648, the territorial principle has been the lynchpin of the Western political system. As Max Weber observed, state territorial sovereignty was identical with control of the monopoly of legitimate violence.[1] Modern political order and law was built on the transcendent power of the state alone to distinguish good violence, or force, from bad violence, or crime within its territorial limits.

In practice, this monopoly was always limited. Until 1914, European states, and their settler colonies, pursued empire by distinguishing "internal frontiers" between the central metropolitan core and the imperial extension. Outside the metropolis, the distinction between law and violence was asserted by what Carl Schmitt called the "state of exception," eliding the legal with the nonlegal and treating decisions that would have been illegal at home as having the force of law outside the metropolitan core.[2] As Hannah

Arendt observed, the boundary between force and violence evaporated in the imperial space into lawlessness.[3]

In Britain and France, the distinction between the core and the empire was given physical expression in the concept of "overseas," translating an exercise in extended power into a mission to civilize, encapsulated as the burden of the white man "to wait in heavy harness on fluttered folk and wild, — your new-caught sullen peoples, half devil and half child."[4]

But in the land empires of Europe, the distinction was less clear-cut. In large parts of the Austro-Hungarian and Ottoman Empires, as well as the margins of Russia and Germany, populations met and "bled into" each other. As literacy and economic transformation spread, central authority began to face organized counterclaims by democratic "nations" to legitimacy. The difference between force and violence and the boundaries between internal and external were increasingly contested.

The decaying Ottoman Empire in the Balkans was the cradle of crisis. But the watershed for imperial legitimacy was World War I. The brutality of imperial war radically undermined the legitimacy of the regimes that prosecuted it but lost. In 1918, Woodrow Wilson confirmed the legitimacy of anti-imperialism among the "subject" peoples of the defeated empires when he made *national self-determination* the central pillar of a just postwar peace:

> What we demand in this war, therefore, is nothing peculiar to ourselves. It is that the world be made fit and safe to live in; and particularly that it be made safe for every peace-loving nation which, like our own, wishes to live its own life, determine its own institutions, be assured of justice and fair dealing by the other peoples of the world as against force and selfish aggression.[5]

But in declaring that free sovereignty over territory was equivalent to national self-assertion, Wilson inevitably transformed territories previously contained within single dynastic territories across Central and Eastern Europe into objects of bitterly contested claims by "national selves." The claims drew variously on a convenient mix of historic claims, modern demographic majorities, or physical contiguity. Territories where sovereignty, and hence the monopoly of legitimate violence, was claimed by more than one nation were transformed into "interfaces" between rival claims, described by Frank Wright as "ethnic frontiers." Was Bohemia a historic indivisible unity, or must it be divided into separate constituent parts by language majorities? Was Slovakia a definable territory at all? And what of the 2.8 million Jews spread across the new Poland?

The Allies in 1918 found that picking national winners automatically implied national losers in many postimperial territories. By definition, these decisions determined the distinction between legitimate and illegitimate violence. In general, the victors resolved dilemmas *against* the defeated central powers while exempting themselves from the principle altogether.[6] The Peace Treaties left the Russians untouched and crushed the ambitions of "lesser winners" in Japan and Italy. Within 20 years, democracy had been replaced by one-party authoritarianisms in Germany, Italy, Russia, and Japan claiming authority outside their allotted territory and rejecting the decisions taken about legitimate violence at Versailles.

THE CRISIS OF NATIONALITY IN IRELAND

Formally, the British Empire, victorious and still expanding in 1918, was unaffected by postwar peace talks. But for 40 years prior to the war, the same issues made Ireland the intractable center of constitutional politics in the United Kingdom. In practice, the contest of postimperial legitimacy that engulfed the postwar world could not be contained to "other people's" territories.

Long before 1914, Ireland had occupied a unique place in the British Empire. While Ireland was in theory core to the unitary imperial state, participating directly in Victorian democratic reforms, Irish politics were marked by what Frank Wright describes as a "crisis of assimilation."[7] As literacy and democracy spread, Ireland voted and agitated distinctively in relation to the imperial center and to the law.

Faced with a resistant "internal-other," Gladstone, the dominant liberal politician of his age, came to the conviction that only Irish self-government in domestic matters could preserve the longer term unity of the United Kingdom and introduced his first "Home Rule" Bill in 1885. But Gladstone's conversion surfaced powerful subterranean conflicts about legitimacy, the British "national" interest, and identity, which ultimately broke both the Liberal Party and the consensus of the British ruling class. It also broke Ireland.

As the transcendence of the imperial state failed in Ireland, it failed unevenly. The territorial locus for this "crisis within a crisis" was in the north of Ireland. Whereas Gladstone and Irish nationalists treated Ireland as a single defined territorial jurisdiction, they underplayed the distinct legacy of empire and industrialization in the northeast. Here, the crisis of assimilation after 1885 revitalized the persistent indigenous political conflict between British state loyalists (Unionists) and Irish nationalists, defined still by religious affiliation.

By relocating the locus of territorial sovereignty from the empire to popular national identity, Home Rule almost instantly crystallized political alignments, modernized the association between imperialism and religious identity, and dynamically accelerated polarization. Proposals to hand power to nationalist Ireland placed the British state in direct opposition to its own most fervently loyal "citizens" on the island, a zeal that opponents of Home Rule were determined to harness. In practice, this meant encouraging the determination of Unionists to resist "betrayal" especially in Ulster where they were economically and territorially dominant. By raising the potential for confrontation between the state and its most fervent loyalists (through what Frank Wright calls "deterrence actions"),[8] the Home Rule question triggered a wider sense of imperial crisis.

When Home Rule became a realistic prospect after 1911, the Unionists raised their cause into an explicitly sacred enterprise, mobilized a large popular militia and threatened armed insurrection. "Humbly relying on God," almost half a million Unionists pledged to use "all means which may be found necessary to defeat the present conspiracy to set up a Home Rule Parliament in Ireland."[9] For this, they received both explicit parliamentary cover from the conservative opposition, including thinly veiled support for righteous violent resistance. By the time of the outbreak of World War I, an escalation to new extremes was underway.

The decisive final straw was the war itself that radicalized nationalism and uprooted the established order everywhere. In the slaughter of the Somme and the heroic failure of the Easter Rising, each side in Ireland had their sacred martyrs and glorious dead. The moderate prodevolution Irish Parliamentary Party had been eclipsed by the revolutionary proindependence politics of Sinn Fein across much of Ireland and in Protestant Ulster, Unionism's wartime loyalty to the imperial cause had reinforced their determination to resist separation from the imperial mothership. A prewar constitutional crisis had escalated into violent confrontation characterized by insurgent terrorism and harsh counterinsurgency. But as part of the victorious British Empire, there was never any prospect that Ireland would be considered at the Paris Peace Conference.

The British government resolved its immediate legitimacy crisis through conceding to the dual logic of "territorial larger forces" and proposed not one but two Home Rule parliaments in Northern and Southern Ireland, both within the United Kingdom. This had the clear advantage of not requiring the British state to confront either party in Ireland by creating a clear Unionist majority in the North and an overwhelming Nationalist majority in the South. Although it met no organized prior demand, the idea of "Northern Ireland" was a desperate pragmatic attempt at managing the increasingly unmanageable, a technocratic constitutional device to bring some administratively enforceable calm in a context of irreconcilable rivals. Its appeal to London was not so much its desirability as its feasibility.

Ironically, Home Rule in this version suited the imperial loyalists but incensed radical Irish nationalism. But while Nationalists could veto devolution in the south, they had no capacity to prevent the establishment of British-backed Unionist domination in the north. When the British conceded greater independence to Ireland only months later, "Northern Ireland" opted out.

VIOLENCE AND TRANSCENDENT ORDER

Wilson intended democracy to free nations from the shackles of imperial domination. Within 20 years East-Central Europe descended into a catastrophe of national rivalry. Under the cloak of self-determination ("*Heim ins Reich*") and challenging the humiliation of the "Versailles traitors," Hitler marched into the Saarland, Austria, and Czechoslovakia. In his obsession to avenge German humiliation at Versailles, self-determination became *lebensraum* and then the *final solution*. Sacred authority was claimed for unspeakable violence in the service of nation. Previously inconceivable ethnic violence, in what Timothy Snyder has called "the Bloodlands," engulfed the resented "national" states between Germany and Russia.[10]

Violence and the sacred is core to the work of René Girard.[11] Girard roots human violence in competing and escalating desires for the same object. The objects of desire do not emerge spontaneously but from emulation or "mimesis" of the desires of others. Human existence is mimetic rather than autonomous, interdependent rather than independent. But because human desire is imitative or "mimetic," it has the tendency to polarize around desire for the same object.

The mimetic qualities of desire mean that the escalating resistance increases fascination. At an unpredictable point, rivalry over an object or possession escalates into direct rivalry with the rival preventing possession and towards violence.

The escalation to mimetic violence is the greatest threat to human survival. Establishing the social order is therefore crucial. Unlike Hobbes, Girard rejects the notion of rational "social contract" as the origin of order in a mimetic frenzy. "Peace" requires a change to the mimetic relationships in the community. Girard hypothesizes that human culture, including the social and religious order, arose from the limitation of violence that could only emerge when violence mimetically converged on a single designated "other." Social peace is the consequence of the violence of "all against one." The rivalry of the community is driven out with its scapegoat.

Crucially, the process, and the violent participation of the mob, remains hidden from its beneficiaries. The miraculous, if paradoxical, peace among the remaining community results from externalizing violence. From within, peace is attributed as the objective action of the scapegoat. Religion and culture recount their origins as "myth": the experience of scapegoating as recounted by its beneficiaries.[12] For Girard, the sacred is revealed as the violence that drove out the scapegoat, a violence that is threatened if the sacred order is transgressed. The community has its peace from internal violence by attributing it "externally" to a divine "other."

The central function of religion and culture is the regulation of internal mimetic violence through prohibitions and taboos and structures and ritual. When cultural order is threatened, cultures and religions intuitively seek peace by directing sacred violence (disguised as force) against an external other. Culture therefore "contains" violence in both senses of contain: Rooted in violence, it contains wider violence.

Modernity stands in a complex relationship to this process. On the one hand, the state is the inheritor of sacred authority as the holder of the monopoly of legitimate violence. On the other, the modern western state stands at the end of a long gradual process during which the origin of the sacred in violence has gradually emerged. Girard attributes the demystification of violence to the extending influence of Judeo-Christianity and, in particular, to the reversal of the scapegoat mechanism in the crucifixion.[13] Violence along with the complicity of the mob is revealed and its sacred claims destroyed. At the same time, Judeo-Christianity strips modernity of the protection of sacred violence against mimetic escalation. Violence exercised in the name of the sacred is increasingly "just violence" and without limitation.

Modernity exhibits an unparalleled sensitivity for victims and to the complicity of social order with violence, including its own. But it has also disarms the sacred transcendence under which the state managed illegitimate violence with legitimate force. Where the force of the state is declared illegitimate, the ability of the state to mediate violence and to establish order disappears. Where legitimacy is claimed for a rival violence, the potential for mimetic escalation is limited only by the balance of forces. Even in the case where the enemy is destroyed, violence achieves no cultural closure. Violence can no longer be hidden. Instead of driving out violence, violence rebounds on its users and generates imitators.

When Woodrow Wilson declared the transcendence of democracy exercised as national self-determination in 1918, many territories became subject to rival claims to a monopoly of violence where the only "control" was the balance of forces. When the borders of legitimacy were actually determined by victors who continued to assert imperial legitimacy in their own territories, they also incensed the truncated and frustrated empires. The distance between a declaration that national self-determination is sovereign and an insistence that violence in service of the nation is legitimate or even obligatory where self-determination is challenged proved to be very short. Everywhere, violence was justified as force in the service of legitimate ends. But the only consistent distinction between force and violence was subjective: "Our" violence is force, and "their" violence is criminal. Violence no longer drove out violence, but escalated it. As Paul Dumouchel observes, "like sacrifice, political violence is a form of violence designed to protect against violence ... it is now unable to protect us from violence or give rise to a stable order."[14]

POLITICAL ANTHROPOLOGY: ETHNIC & RELIGIOUS MINORITIES

RIVALRY AND ORDER IN THE ETHNIC FRONTIER

"Empire loyalists" in ethnically contested areas of Austria-Hungary and Germany found themselves minorities in new national challenger-states where territory was contested. The lost territories in the east were transformed into evidence of the humiliation of the German nation at Versailles. As Paul Dumouchel observes: "we no longer have the territorial order, a continuous isotropic space of which each part is external to each other."[15]

Escalated international territorial rivalry had direct consequences for the internal politics of the new states. Where there was an unredeemed minority now under foreign authority, domestic policy was aligned to foreign policy. Where an internal "other" emerged, politics relied on vigilance. Where one part of its (internal) population was regarded as an (external) threat, the law became part of the process of pre-emption and escalation. Rivalry over sovereignty was reflected in systemic inequality, deepening resentment. The exercise by the state of its monopoly of legitimate force resembled the opposition it confronted, eroding, and eventually eliminating, the distinction between force and violence on which the law relies for its monopoly.

Wright characterizes the resulting relationship as endemic "*antagonism*," defined as "being on different sides of a force [and violence] relationship."[16] The path of conflict in the ethnic frontier is measured less by the possession of specific objects than by ensuring advantage in the mimetic rivalry itself. Politics is about relativities rather than absolutes change. As Frank Wright points out, "Antagonism (mimetic rivalry) is more fundamental than all the various 'things' the antagonism keeps for the dominant and denies to the dominated."[17] Potentially anything that threatens the balance of power can trigger hostility. Crucially, conflict cannot be "resolved" simply by establishing frameworks of formal equality around "things" for as long as the mimetic suspicion remains intact.

Political relationships in a force field are simultaneously characterized by hostility between rivals and internal group solidarity. Violence, or the threat of violence, is simultaneously fascinating and polarizing (alienating). Group identity becomes critical as violence becomes "representative." An attack on one member of a group is experienced as an attack on the whole group, while all members of "the others" are implicitly complicit in any violence. Vengeance can potentially be taken against any identified member. Relationships between individuals are increasingly conducted *within* the wider mimetic antagonism. Ultimately, groups have their collective identity vis-à-vis an ideologically *singular* "them," which is simultaneously everywhere. Directing violence in the name of vigilance, deterrence and suspicion become the highest virtues of patriotism.

Technical categories such as "citizenship" must be parsed in practice into friends and foes, institutionalizing suspicion and inequality at the heart of all processes of state. Equality is rendered implausible by the need to have a pre-emptive advantage over a rival terror. Peace without victory is tantamount to surrender, equivalent to trusting a Trojan horse. Even an "absence of violence" in which the relationship of antagonism remains untouched is experienced as a truce.

Wright demonstrates that the crucial differences between Eastern Europe and Ireland lay in the external environment. The crisis of rival claims to self-determination was resolved by creating Northern Ireland *inside* the old imperial state. By determining its own process of exit from empire, Britain avoided the humiliation of international dictation. By upholding the position of empire loyalists where they lived in territorially defensible numbers, immediate political risk to the state subsided. Voluntary disengagement all but eliminated British interest in Ireland. The novel device of devolving all power over domestic policy to the local majority in Northern Ireland confined the contest of nationality that had defined British–Irish relations since the 1840s into the new "province."

While the Irish Free State was territorially truncated, the new state was born without significant internal minority resistance. Partition ensured that the national struggle was elsewhere, confined overwhelmingly *within* the new Northern Ireland. As the remnant Protestant community was slowly assimilated, anti-Britishness became a constitutional obligation rather than an immediate priority.

More gradually, the evident inability of independent Ireland to change the partition settlement limited the fascination of the "unredeemed" fourth green field.

In Girardian terms, Northern Ireland's distinct territorial identity and the inability of Ireland to effect change through violence reduced, but could not eliminate, the level of external mimetic rivalry over the contested territory. The "rest of Britain" and, eventually, "the rest of Ireland" "externalized" and slowly moderated their own historic hostility.

But the national dispute was not so much resolved as "contained" and concentrated into Northern Ireland. Neither integrated into the imperial homeland nor an independent nation state, Northern Ireland became, in Wright's description, an institutionalized "ethnic frontier."

Historically, "a place between," the north of Ireland was now "a place apart" in a permanent "state of exception." Territorial legitimacy, presumed elsewhere in Britain and Ireland, was endemically at risk. Rival claims to sovereignty and legitimacy defined the single axis of division between vigilant "supporters" and actively hostile "rejectionists" of the new arrangements.

Unionist attempts to assert the monopoly of violence by the state could not be separated from their endemic insecurity. Security depended on maintaining the fragile balance of forces. Elections measured the balance with no expectation of change. With a Unionist monopoly on power, Nationalist hostility to the state shaded into sympathy for resistance, while Unionists developed the legal framework for permanent emergency law despite their parliamentary monopoly. In this, Northern Ireland almost exactly matched Dumouchel's description:

> It is important to remember that the reign of suspicion is the contrary to the rule of law.... Foes are rendered inoffensive, incapable of doing harm, before they are able to act. The object is not justice, which seeks to maintain a degree of proportion between the crime and the punishment, but efficiency at the cost of a few "unfortunate mistakes."... Suspicion is to law what a pre-emptive strike is to a declaration of war.[18]

The cycle of antagonism ultimately impinged on every relationship, embedded in politics, residence, employment practices, policing, education, arts and sport, and local government. Almost none of this was officially acknowledged. Yet, for as long as actual violence remained suppressed, the state presented itself as uncontested. Only the permanent existence of emergency legislation told otherwise.

FROM CONTAINMENT TO ESCALATION TO CONTAINMENT?

Northern Ireland's political balance collapsed in the late 1960s. In western Europe, the alliance against communism and political cooperation had established an unexpected degree of territorial stability. After 1945, Britain exited empire almost by stealth, presenting decline as a newfound commitment to "self-determination," albeit on the random boundaries of imperial conquest. Ominously, decolonization was most violent where the descendants of imperial settlements violently resisted a future as resented minorities, such as Southern Africa and French Algeria. Here, settlers found themselves repudiated as uniquely racist dinosaurs. The western powers presented liberal democracy as progressive inevitability, as natural now as it had been precarious in the 1930s.

Meanwhile, Ireland and Britain reached an unspoken *modus vivendi*. Both states formally restated their claims to sovereignty Northern Ireland in the 1940s but both were increasingly focused on joining the European Economic Community. Neither showed any sign of wishing to wake the sleeping dog.

The speed of escalation in violence in Northern Ireland demonstrated that it was not only the dog that was asleep. When demands for full civil rights and an end to discrimination against Catholics met significant Unionist opposition in the late 1960s, violence erupted on an unprecedented scale, it appeared to catch Dublin and London unprepared. Rioting escalated into confrontation between the police and civil rights protesters and intercommunity violence. The crisis of the 1920s was evoked in the reappearance of groups claiming a historic legitimacy for violence.

As violence escalated at an alarming rate, the underpinning crisis of legitimacy was re-exposed. Both governments found themselves rapidly drawn back into the crisis. With British acquiescence, the Northern Ireland government activated the emergency powers legislation and introduced internment without trial. But instead of restoring order, the legitimacy of the state in Northern Ireland now faced international scrutiny. Inexorably, the British state was being drawn into direct confrontation with Irish Nationalism. Within six months, the British army was being internationally condemned for shooting civilians on the street. Meanwhile, members of the Irish government were sacked for allegedly arranging for arms to be smuggled into Northern Ireland. The Irish government pleaded with UN to send peacekeepers.

But given that Northern Irish politics was conducted as mortal combat over belonging to Ireland or Britain, the most striking aspect of Northern Ireland is its survival as a separate political entity. The isolation of the political priorities of Northern Ireland by partition/devolution had decisively weakened national solidarity. To an exceptional extent, violence in Northern Ireland failed to rouse the majority of the population in either Britain or Ireland to action. The British press explained the conflict not in historic British–Irish terms but as an incomprehensible "religious war" between remnant "Catholics and Protestants."

Meanwhile, despite the explicit constitutional claim to sovereignty over the whole of Ireland, the crisis in the North merely emphasized the inability of the Irish state to do anything practical about the border. In practice, both governments acted to limit themselves against the risk of being drawn into a national conflict that their voters now regarded as "little to do with us."

Containing violence became the key priority. The need to avoid being drawn into deeper antagonism meant controlling the response of the state, forcing the British State to intervene directly. In March 1972, to Unionist fury, Northern Ireland's devolved parliament was summarily abolished as "a temporary measure." At the same time, both governments made very clear that they regarded this as temporary. Northern Ireland's distinct arm's length special status was explicitly retained. The Irish government introduced its own draconian measures to isolate anyone advocating violence south of the border. The governments actively cooperated in a desperate attempt to negotiate voluntary power-sharing deal for Northern Ireland in 1973.

But when the experiment in power-sharing collapsed after five months in the face of mass protests by Unionists, the British government was left to administer Northern Ireland alone. Republican demands for British withdrawal and Unionist proposals to restore the principle of majority-rule were rejected, but power-sharing remained impossible. Instead, the British government pursued "the acceptable level of violence" and a "normalization" of law and order through a combination of massive army presence, commitments to address inequality and physical separation "peace walls." Superior military force gradually restricted violence into segregated, often poor, urban areas where paramilitary organizations had active support and rural districts with continuous traditions of struggles for land and power in a long, grinding "war of attrition." Meanwhile, England, Scotland, and Wales were protected *from* Northern Ireland by means of the Prevention of Terrorism Act.

THE PROCESS OF PEACE?

Overwhelming force could protect minimum order but not create legitimacy. When the British government withdrew the special status granted to prisoners arrested for political and terror offenses, republican prisoners starved themselves to death in defiance of the attempt to "label our liberation struggle as criminal."[19] The "martyrdom" of the hunger strikes polarized the population, rejuvenated Irish republicanism and underlined both the sacred intensity of the demand for Irish self-determination and the limits of the law's ability to assert a monopoly of legitimate violence.

In 1982, Britain was galvanized by the "humiliation" of the Argentinian invasion of the Falkland Islands into a frenzy of national outrage. Yet, in the face of apparently endless violence at the same time, Northern Ireland was, more than ever, distanced as "other." Territorial ambition was reduced to historic obligation and to "containing" the crisis in Northern Ireland.

The prospects for British disengagement or ending hostilities seemed evermore distant. In an atmosphere approaching despair, both governments edged towards cooperation. The Anglo-Irish Agreement that emerged in 1985 proved to be the most radical recalibration of intergovernmental relationships in Ireland since 1920. Without repudiating historic commitments, the governments framed their desire to contain and manage violence within an ill-defined commitment to "reconciliation." Peace in Northern Ireland could not be won by asserting one nationality over the other but by renouncing violence. Implicitly, and in contrast to official constitutional theory, both governments were edging towards a supranational transcendence that drew an international antithesis between the rule of law informed by international norms and all other violence, terror, or antagonism. By placing the denationalized "victims of violence" at the center, violence in pursuit of national self-determination was abandoned. Patriotism now implied accommodation with, rather than the destruction of, the national enemy.

The consequences were not immediately clear, or even intended by the signatories. Joint sovereignty had been explicitly ruled out. However, the UK government conceded a special role to Ireland for safeguarding equality of treatment and raising security concerns in Northern Ireland and established a joint British–Irish secretariat to liaise between the governments and regular meetings over Northern Ireland between the British Secretary of State and the Irish Foreign Minister in exchange for security cooperation and a restatement of the position that Irish unity would not take place without the consent of the majority in Northern Ireland. Underpinning this, the agreement established a new "International Fund for Ireland" (IFI) to invest in economic regeneration and reconciliation across the island of Ireland, financed by donations from the United States, the Commonwealth, and the European Union.

In Northern Ireland, reaction to the abandonment of national solidarity was immediate and dramatic. Enraged Unionists demonstrated and agitated in a total mobilization against the new deal. Republicans reacted with horror against the "nationalist nightmare." Imported arms and munitions from the eastern bloc, Libya, and South Africa kept the street war alive and there was no immediate decrease in the level of murderous violence. Both were alive with accusations of betrayal and abandonment. But despite continuing atrocity, no party could create significant external political momentum against the agreement. Critically, the key axis of negotiation was with the Anglo–Irish framework, not between the Northern Irish antagonists.

Reconciliation was in effect a new transcendence in British–Irish affairs and a political framework that governments applied strictly to Northern Ireland. The fact that the British and Irish states set limits to their willingness to uphold self-determination in Northern Ireland was a product of Northern Ireland's "otherness." Although the policy was ostensibly focused on building relationships *between* Northern Ireland's warring factions, it had to be pursued *against* all of their instincts.

The moderation of nationalism by reconciliation was a remarkable political development. Northern Ireland's isolation from the mainstream of British and Irish politics ensured that decades of mimetic violence over the territorial sovereignty and the monopoly of violence did not galvanize Britain and Ireland into war. Instead, in the face of years of attempting to pacify and manage, the overwhelming lesson was the hopelessness of violence. In addressing violence, reconciliation was not an admission of national defeat but the last best hope of preventing the escalation to the extremes. Furthermore, in the context of postwar liberal democracy, by establishing an international ethical framework it modified the imperative of national self-determination and created the international context within which a territorial monopoly of violence could be exercised.

In real political terms, nationalists of every sort were now confronted by the overwhelming combined forces of the nations they purported to defend. Paradoxically, the only question was the extent to which "reconciliation" would have to be externally "enforced" or whether it could be adopted by negotiation. For the governments, the primary goal was the devolution of responsibility for reconciliation to the parties in Northern Ireland, ensuring that its volatile antagonism was contained. For the local protagonists, engagement in the peace process was primarily necessary to limit further abandonment, only possible by substituting their own agreement for those between governments.

It was clear to everyone that this would require facing a future where antagonists shared power on the basis of equality. Much more problematically, however, it also implied that violence in pursuit of "our" cause would be regarded as equivalent to violence pursued by "our enemies," an acknowledgement that no party, including governments, was willing to make.

Over 12 years, in a multidimensional series of negotiations collectively known as the "peace process," governments and parties tiptoed into fundamental negotiations. Communication was reestablished with Unionists by the late 1980s. By 1994, the key paramilitary antagonists agreed to cease-fires. American diplomacy and European finance increased the room for manoeuver and widened community momentum for change beyond political parties. Despite a boycott by radical Unionism around Ian Paisley's Democratic Unionists (DUP), the governments established talks in 1997 that concluded with the Belfast or Good Friday Agreement (GFA) in April 1998.

BETWEEN RIVALRY AND RECONCILIATION

The political centerpiece of efforts to establish the transcendence for reconciliation was the Good Friday Agreement. This was established unambiguously in the second paragraph of the text:

> The tragedies of the past have left a deep and profoundly regrettable legacy of suffering. We must never forget those who have died or been injured, and their families. But we can best honour them through a fresh start, in which we firmly dedicate ourselves to the achievement of reconciliation, tolerance, and mutual trust, and to the protection and vindication of the human rights of all.[20]

Taken literally, this amounts to the renunciation of one relationship for another by all signatories, including those from Northern Ireland. Furthermore, all parties explicitly affirmed their "absolute and total commitment to exclusively democratic and peaceful means of resolving differences on political issues"[21] and accepted that it was "essential to acknowledge and address the suffering of the victims of violence as a necessary element of reconciliation."[22]

Reconciliation and nonviolence were underpinned by an emphasis on international human rights law (which no law can infringe) and statutory equality. Most dramatically of all, the Good Friday Agreement severed the link between territorial sovereignty and unique citizenship, reconfiguring national identity as a matter of choice between equals rather than sacred obligation:

> [T]he birthright of all the people of Northern Ireland to identify themselves and be accepted as Irish or British, or both, as they may so choose, and accordingly confirm that their right to hold both British and Irish citizenship is accepted by both Governments and would not be affected by any future change in the status of Northern Ireland.[23]

But if political responsibility was to be devolved, there was no way to avoid doing a deal with antagonism. Yet, by setting "reconciliation" against traditional national goals, it was turned into the measure of *defeat* for Northern Ireland's recalcitrant antagonists. If reconciliation was concession, protecting communal antagonism was a success. The consequences of this have proved profound.

The political deal that emerged in 1998 was a complex hybrid. The signatories reaffirmed the formal sovereignty of Irish self-determination while accepting that a united Ireland could only be achieved "with and subject to the agreement and consent of a majority of the people of Northern Ireland."[24] Power-sharing in Northern Ireland was made mandatory, North-South cooperation on identified issues was institutionalized and a new British-Irish Council was established to bring together the various elected institutions of "the islands" in a largely consultative forum. Equality of opportunity was to be enhanced and regulated through an Equality Commission and public life was to be pursued within a framework of "parity of esteem" between nationalism and unionism.

But within Northern Ireland, the structures were strictly consociational. Ministerial posts were assigned proportionally to party strength creating a coalition emphasizing participation by right. Members of the Legislative Assembly (MLAs) designated as Unionist, Nationalist, or "other," because a number of votes required "parallel consent." Groups of 30 MLAs could raise "petitions of concern" vetoing measures without cross-community consent.

More significantly, the negotiators relied on ambiguity to close the deal on a number of critical issues. The most incendiary was related to "violence connected to the affairs of Northern Ireland," including the release of prisoners, disclosure of state activity, the vindication of victims, and the disbanding and disarmament of paramilitary organizations. Thus, prisoners were released before the end of their sentences but without amnesty. Governments signed up to human rights but without specific commitments to truth-telling. Victims were acknowledged with only vague further promises and disarmament depended on voluntary action by groups who were only indirectly represented at the talks. In contrast, the need for policing reform was recognized, and handed over to an Independent Commission on Policing, which reported in 1999,[25] leaving it to be imposed by the international coalition despite inevitable Unionist and republican objection.

The controlling dynamic of Northern Ireland since 1998 became the interaction between the recognition of the impossibility of violence and the unresolved logic of mimetic national antagonism.

TRUCE OR TRANSFORMATION?

In 1985, Britain and Ireland concluded that the decisive challenges in Northern Ireland were violence and the escalation of conflict. Legitimacy and the rule of law depended on the transcendence of international solidarity against killing over national self-determination. By placing the renunciation of violence over the claims of national egotism, they made one of the most innovative interventions in international relations since 1918 and incurred the hostility of most of the direct political antagonists in Northern Ireland itself.

The symbolism of Good Friday seemed to reinforce the connection between the crucifixion and the strategic emphasis on the victims of violence. Although supported by 70% in the referendum in Northern Ireland, the residual dynamics of reciprocal antagonism almost destroyed the agreement over the next five years. Ambiguity in the rules of disarmament unraveled making it impossible for pro-agreement Unionists to commit to devolved government without risking electoral annihilation. Failure to secure devolved government prevented moderate Nationalists advocating unambiguously for disarmament. Community relations were seriously strained when loyalist protesters in North Belfast attacked children and parents on their way to a Catholic Primary school. In 2002, the crisis of trust over disarmament escalated to the point that the devolved government collapsed and the British governments reinstituted direct rule. Elections in 2003 destroyed the political base of the parties at the core of the Good Friday Agreement to the benefit of the political party most closely identified with unbending hostility.

In effect, antagonism in Northern Ireland forced the government to resume responsibility for reconciliation. The political compromise implementing "reconciliation" of trading devolved responsibility for managed antagonism had fallen apart. The governments and the international community had no alternative but to continue, but they did so increasingly reluctantly. Westminster passed legislation to implement Patten's policing reforms (supported enthusiastically by the Irish and US governments, the Catholic Church, and the Gaelic Athletic Association but accepted with great reluctance by the Unionist parties in Northern Ireland and rejected by Sinn Fein) and introduced a comprehensive strategy for community relations and reforms to equality law without local political support. Meanwhile, huge European and US financial support maintained popular participation in "reconciliation."

But increasingly, the governments were only interested in establishing devolved government. In practice, this meant both defining reconciliation *as* devolution and renegotiating reconciliation with parties that were historically more committed to exclusive versions of national legitimacy to achieve devolution. Ambivalence around decommissioning was resolved especially when US objection to Irish Republican Army killings and a bank robbery forced a process of visible decommissioning. To entice the parties, the governments unilaterally recast aspects of the agreement at St. Andrews to reduce the level of integrated leadership and to reinforce communal separation of the devolved assembly,[26] but other aspects of reconciliation and the agreement, such as commitment to integrated education, intercommunity relations, or developing equality, establishing a civic forum or bill of rights were essentially set aside and with them any necessary evolution away from national separation.

The dramatic reward was agreement by both Sinn Fein and DUP to enter a historic pact to govern Northern Ireland in 2007, greeted with genuine surprise across the world. Devolution instantly removed the UK government from direct political responsibility for most of Northern Ireland's internal affairs with the exception of reserved matters and the still contentious issue of policing and justice. The meaning of reconciliation in practice now depended on the extent to which the new political relationship could contain or transform the underlying rivalry.

AFTER RECONCILIATION: TRUCE AND TRANSFORMATION IN NORTHERN IRELAND SINCE 2007

In effect, the British and Irish governments made clear that the heavy lifting in relation to establishing a territorially viable state, including the monopoly of the legitimacy, was completed by devolution in 2007. A number of obvious things remained to be achieved — including the devolution of policing and justice — but the intergovernmental doctrine was now that the remaining decisions towards reconciliation should be taken in Northern Ireland.

In the years that followed, the transformation of relationships between Britain and Ireland was formally underlined. The state visit of Queen Elizabeth II to Ireland in May 2011 was hailed as a "spectacular diplomatic triumph."[27] Likewise the reciprocal state visit of President Higgins to Britain in April 2014 was described as a cultural "catharsis."[28]

The new Northern Ireland administration initially sought to focus on issues of common interest — primarily economic — rather than resolving contentious issues. But as the global financial crisis rendered hopes of an economic dividend implausible, so the evidence of unresolved antagonism resurfaced.

As a variety of triggers escalated into more general disputes about the balance of power, the executive repeatedly polarized and looked for external support. Agreeing arrangements for policing and justice required the direct reintervention of the British, Irish, and US governments in 2010. The final deal managed the unique challenges of administering common justice in a society characterized by hostile suspicion by removing the new ministry from the consociational proportionality arrangements, allocating it uniquely to a minister with cross-community support. In 2012, serious rioting broke out when the Belfast City Council reduced the number of days the union flag was flown on City Hall. In 2013, disputes over single parade routes, escalated into confrontation. When an internal dispute among republicans spilled into assassinations in 2015, Unionists called time on normal political business.

Despite a marked reduction in the level of overt violence, paramilitary activity continued and police and prison officers lived under a continuing death threat. Meanwhile, the executive made slow progress on removing the so-called peacelines or reducing residential segregation and seemed to step back from integrated education. Attempts to extend equality or to promote a Bill of Rights fell on the rock of intercommunity division while promises to devise a policy to improve community relations took six years to materialize, driven in the end by the need to demonstrate to an international audience at the G8 that Northern Ireland was indeed making progress.

Yet, against this, shared government followed a distinct pattern of survival. Disputes *between* the rival groups in Northern Ireland escalated until the point that only external mediation could break the impasse, at which point the reluctant governments accepted the need to intervene. Talks also took on an identifiable arc as all parties appeared to wait until the last possible moment to make decisions, conceding only when it was clear that the alternative was a total collapse in the system. Clearly, escalating rivalry towards violence in Northern Ireland remained a risk, yet all parties appeared to accept that only shared government and nonviolence could provide any way forward. More problematically, however, the parties appeared to have made little progress at making concessions to one another on issues of antagonism and continued to rely on the mediation and resources of governments.

TERRITORIALITY, POLITICS, AND VIOLENCE IN NORTHERN IRELAND

For Rene Girard, human efforts to contain violence have reached a critical juncture. Drawing on von Clausewitz's dictum that war has "the form of a dual" and a tendency to escalate to the extremes.[29] Girard rejects Hegel's optimism that dialectical conflict leads to universal *Aufhebung*. Because violence cannot be checked by superior violence, violence has an unprecedented capacity to escalate rapidly to the extremes. "Violence can no longer be checked. From this point of view we can say that the apocalypse has begun.... In a more realistic manner than Hegel, Clausewitz showed the utter powerlessness of politics against the escalation to extremes. Ideological wars, monstrous justifications of violence, have led humanity to the stage beyond war where we are today."[30]

Since 1918, the dynamic of national self-determination, especially in territories where no single nation can prevail without violence, illustrates the modern dilemma. The collapse of the imperial in the face of a politics of liberty, becomes enmeshed in mimetic rivalry over territorial control, rendering the whole notion of territory, as a cornerstone of global order increasingly unable to manage violence. Instead of the monopoly of legitimate violence, every rival claims legitimacy for their violence. Where a balance of forces cannot be established or the intervention of outside powers transforms local ethnic violence into international conflict, the result is potentially lethal for international affairs.

The question of whether politics has any response to this challenge is therefore urgent. In this regard, the emergence in Northern Ireland of "reconciliation" as a framework for international ethical norms beyond national self-determination was especially significant. The prioritization of an obligation to victims over the demands of national ascendancy represents a potentially important illustration of the capacity to arrest the escalation to the extremes through the renunciation of violence.

At the same time, it is evident that the gap between reconciliation and mimetic rivalry remains unclosed. In many ways, the commitment of the British and Irish governments to reconciliation in Northern Ireland can be attributed to their relative indifference to the outcome and their unusual distance from its polarized mimetic dynamics. As a consequence, the British and Irish governments were not confronted with the need to renounce their own position but called on a smaller "other," in this case Northern Ireland, to do so. In spite of the huge amount of money spent on resolving conflict, however, the outcome has been ambivalent. On the one hand, the antagonism of Northern Ireland has clearly entered a new less violent chapter. At the same time, it has proved impossible to simply renounce the impulse to mimetic escalation or hostility.

The challenges to reconciliation in the future proved to be most acute in relation to violence in the past. In its focus on a new start, the Good Friday Agreement left untouched whether violence on behalf of self-determination prior to 1998 was or was not legitimate.

Violence in Northern Ireland's deep-rooted ecosystem of antagonism escaped simple definitions of crime and war, leaving a legacy of widespread ambivalence about violence, unacknowledged complicity and contested categories of heroism and criminality and contrasting experiences of the rule of law. Both the Good Friday Agreement and the Patten Commission eschewed any formal reckoning with history in favor of a "New Beginning." Both elevated the memorability of "innocent victims of violence" but left hanging the reciprocal Girardian movement of the revelation of complicity.

But it quickly became apparent that drawing a line was impossible in the face of the social and cultural legacy of violence and the demands of international human rights law. It was equally clear that justice administered through normal legal processes would be both contested and increasingly difficult as time passed. Above all, political parties were wedded to particular narratives of crime and heroism that could be undermined by certain processes and vindicated by others. Despite an early release program, victims support schemes, inquiries, coronial inquests, ombudsman investigations, and a full-scale commission,[31] nobody was willing to expose their complicity with violence at the cost of losing control of the moral economy. What remained was a culture of accusation and counteraccusation and exposure by journalistic investigation. The price of ending mimetic rivalry that nobody seemed willing to face remained the question of acknowledging participation in violence and taking responsibility for restoring relationships.

"Reconciliation" has made an important contribution to the search for a new politics of legitimacy in a divided society. Yet, until now the mimetic fragility of relationships in Northern Ireland was reinforced by the growing confidence of relationships between London and Dublin. It remains to be seen whether reconciliation between Britain and Ireland will survive Brexit. The Northern Ireland peace project remains a work in progress. Girard's challenge to politics remains unresolved.

NOTES

1. Max Weber, "Politik als Beruf," in Max Weber, ed., *Gesammelte Politische Schriften* (Munich: Duncker & Humboldt, 1924), 396–450.
2. Giorgio Agamben, *State of Exception* (Chicago: University of Chicago Press, 2005), 23.
3. Hannah Arendt, *The Origins of Totalitarianism* (New York: Schocken Books, 1951), 231.
4. Rudyard Kipling, "The White Man's Burden," in Rudyard Kipling, ed., *Complete Poems* (London: Wordsworth, 2001), 334.
5. See Transcript of Woodrow Wilson's Fourteen Points (1918), https://www.ourdocuments.gov/doc.php?doc=62&page=transcript (accessed 12 September 2016).
6. Margaret MacMillan, *Peacemakers* (London: John Murray, 2001).
7. Frank Wright, *Northern Ireland: A Comparative Analysis* (Dublin and London: Gill and MacMillan, 1987), 1–11.
8. Ibid., 11–50.
9. Gordon Lucy, *The Ulster Covenant: A Pictorial History of the 1912 Home Rule Crisis* (Newtownards, Northern Ireland: Ulster Society/Colourpoint, 2012), 1.
10. Timothy Snyder, *Bloodlands: Europe Between Hitler and Stalin* (London: Vintage, 1910).
11. Rene Girard, *Violence and the Sacred* (Baltimore, MD: Johns Hopkins University Press, 1977).
12. Ibid., 271.
13. Rene Girard, *Things Hidden Since the Foundation of the World* (London: The Athlone Press, 1987), 180–223.
14. Paul Dumouchel, *The Barren Sacrifice* (East Lansing, MI: Michigan State University Press, 2015), xxxii.
15. Ibid., 166.
16. Wright, "Northern Ireland," xiii.
17. Ibid., 220.

18. Dumouchel, "The Barren Sacrifice," 167.
19. Bobby Sands, *Writings from Prison* (Cork: Mercier Press, 1983), 225.
20. See Belfast Agreement (1998), paragraph 2, https://www.dfa.ie/media/dfa/alldfawebsitemedia/ourrolesandpolicies/northernireland/good-friday-agreement.pdf. (accessed 16 Nov. 2016).
21. Ibid., paragraph 4.
22. Ibid., paragraph 11.
23. Ibid., Constitutional Issues, 1(vi).
24. Ibid., Article 1 (ii).
25. Independent Commission on Policing for Northern Ireland, *A New Beginning: Policing in Northern Ireland* (London and Belfast: Her Majesty's Stationery Office, 1999).
26. See St. Andrews Agreement (2006), https://www.gov.uk/government/uploads/system/uploads/attachment_data/file/136651/st_andrews_agreement-2.pdf (accessed 15 Nov. 2016).
27. "The Queen in Ireland: Standing Ovation in Dublin," *Daily Telegraph*, 20 May 2011.
28. "The Irish state visit was a piece of public theatre, but also a catharsis," *The Guardian*, 11 April 2014.
29. Carl von Clausewitz, *On War* (Princeton: Princeton University Press, 1976), 75.
30. Rene Girard, *Battling to the End* (East Lansing MI: Michigan State University Press, 2010), 209–210.
31. See Robin Eames and Denis Bradley, *Report of the Consultative Group on the Past* (2009), http://cain.ulst.ac.uk/victims/docs/consultative_group/cgp_230109_report.pdf (accessed 9 Oct. 2016).

"In the Margins of Europe": Cypriot Nationalism, Liminality, and the Moral Economy of the Financial Crisis

VASSOS ARGYROU

This article argues that Greek Cypriot nationalism has been in large part motivated by the misconceived idea of Cyprus becoming a modern, European society. Although Cyprus joined the European Union in 2004, the perception of it by the European north as a culturally marginal Mediterranean society had not changed. This was amply demonstrated in 2013 when Cyprus applied to the EU for urgent financial assistance. It was forced to capitalize its banks through their customers' savings and, although this and other "corrective" measures were couched in seemingly rational economic terms, they were unmistakably a punishment and a civilizational lesson.

In his ethnography of village life in Egypt, Amitav Ghosh, the Indian anthropologist and well-known novelist, describes a quarrel with the local Imam for whom the Indian practice of "burning the dead" and "worshiping cows" were signs of a primitive condition. Having argued with him bitterly as to whose country was more "modern and civilized," it finally dawned on Ghosh that he and the Imam had much in common. "At that moment, despite the vast gap that lay between us, we understood each other perfectly. We were both travelling, he and I: we were travelling in the West."[1]

One of the contentions of this article is that this is also the case with the longstanding conflict between Greek and Turkish Cypriots. Although it may appear to be ethnically motivated and religiously based, the roots of the conflict are thoroughly cultural, understood in this broad anthropological sense of the distinction between the West and the other and the presumed superiority of the former over the latter. Greek and Turkish Cypriots as well as mainland Greeks and Turks have been travelling in the West, which is to say, they have been striving to become like the West, supposedly "modern" and "civilized." A second and perhaps more controversial contention is that this is a Sisyphian task, a never-ending journey as there is no such destination to be reached or condition to be appropriated. The West, as much as the notion of modernity itself, is simply an idea or, to put it more strongly and provocatively, a figment of the imagination. There is no such entity that exists in and of itself; to the extent that such an entity exists and is itself, it is only in relation to something not itself, a discredited but nonetheless indispensable other. To be, it must be West of an East, another point arbitrarily chosen on a circle that turns constantly and knows nothing of beginning and end, east or west—a circle on which every point can be both beginning and end, as good an east as a west. Without an Orient then, the West would lose its orientation and disappear in thin air.[2] This means that it pays all those who imagine themselves as the West and wish to be something rather than nothing to maintain an Orient at all costs—sometimes, as we shall see shortly, as a source of inspiration and even a tool with which to critique the West.

Much of this is of course well known. What seems to have received less attention is the predicament of all those societies—which is most, if not all societies around the world—travelling in the West. They become liminal—the third contention of this article—which is to say, entities that are neither here nor there, neither this nor that. They get caught "between and betwixt" what they themselves reject for not being "modern and civilized"—the East—and what rejects them for not being "modern and civilized"—the West.[3] What is perhaps even less discussed is that this predicament befalls also societies in the European periphery, "the margins of Europe,"[4] such as Cyprus—a case of the marginal becoming liminal. This is the case even when the marginal appears to have merged with the center, as Cyprus had done in 2004 when it joined the European Union. Yet, the country is now no less peripheral and marginal than it has ever been for the simple reason that without a periphery there can be no center. And there should be no doubt: Europe posits a center for itself and is determined to maintain it.

The aim of this article is to demonstrate these claims by exploring the recent history of Cyprus and an even more recent event—a "haircut"—the moral economy of the recapitalization of the Cypriot banks by means of their clients' deposits as the condition imposed by the European Union for saving the country from defaulting.

TRAVELING IN THE WEST

Part travel book and part novel, Lawrence Durrell's *Bitter Lemons of Cyprus* describes his short sojourn on the island in search of inspiration and, once there, also as a civil servant in the employ of the colonial a government. The time was 1957 and the Greek Cypriot struggle against the British—in essence, a struggle to liberate Cyprus from British rule and bring it under Greek rule—was in full swing. Anti-British sentiment was running high but even so one of Durrell's close friends, a Greek Cypriot nationalist teacher, could still argue that, in reality, Greek Cypriots loved the British. There is a paradox here, no doubt—in fact, there are two paradoxes and I will turn to the second shortly. If Greek Cypriots loved the British, why fight them? Was this man lying or talking nonsense? Hardly. There is no doubt that Cypriots—both Greek and Turkish—genuinely admired the British. They admired them to such an extent as to want to become like them. And if Durrell is to be believed, to a large extent, they had succeeded. Durrell came to Cyprus looking for inspiration. He was looking for the exotic but what he found was deeply disappointing.

> Disturbing *anomalies* met the eye everywhere; a Cypriot version of the small-car owner, for example, smoking a pipe and reverently polishing a Morris Minor; costumed peasants buying tinned food and frozen meat at the local version of the Co-op.... As far as I could judge the townsman's standard of living roughly corresponded to that of a Manchester suburb.... Somewhere, I concluded, there are must be a Cyprus beyond the red pillar-boxes and the stern Union Jacks ... where *weird* enclaves of these Mediterranean folk lived a joyous, *uproarious, muddled, anarchic* life of their own. Where? [emphases added][5]

The life that Durrell witnessed in Cyprus in the late 1950s was not "proper" Cypriot life, which is to say, not exotic, Mediterranean, Middle Eastern enough. It was disturbingly familiar, a version of the kind of life that one could encounter in a Manchester suburb. Greek Cypriots fought the British, then, not because they did not like them but precisely because they liked them so much as to want to be just like them, especially in certain important respects the British would not allow. The fundamental problem here was the same as in the rest of the colonized world. As Chakrabarty points out in the case of India, the British preached freedom to Indians but refused to grant it in practice.[6] They argued that Indians were not yet mature enough to govern themselves. It is for freedom also that Greek Cypriots fought the British even though the picture in this case is rather more complex—which brings me to the second paradox. Cyprus is probably the only colonized land to have fought against colonial rule not to become independent but part of another country.[7] Greek Cypriots fought the British because they wanted Cyprus to become part of Greece. A textbook case of nationalism, one might say. Perhaps, but the paradox of fighting against one rule only to come freely and willingly under another should not be ignored. If anything, it must be sharpened. To say that the Greek Cypriot desire is a manifestation of nationalist sentiments may be true but explains very little. To understand *why* Greek Cypriots wanted to become part of Greece we must examine two parallel and complementary processes in a specific historical context. The context is the invention of ancient Greece as the cradle of (European) civilization, the Europeanization of Greeks, which meant first and foremost their de-Ottomanization.[8]

Greece was an Ottoman province for almost four centuries and gained its independence in the early 19th century. By that time, ancient Greece had been firmly established in the European imagination as the cradle of (European) civilization so much so that some of the more romantically inclined Europeans actually went to Greece and fought in the Greek war of independence—notable among them Lord Byron. For such people, it was inconceivable that the land that gave birth to democracy, philosophy, theatre, and so on was under "oriental" rule. Much the same can be said about many educated Greeks who lived aboard and were deeply influenced by the Enlightenment and the French Revolution, notable among them, as Anderson notes, Adamantios Koraes.[9] The descendants of the ancient Greeks, the people who had just gained their independence, were nothing like western Europeans. Yet this, according to the nationalist, Eurocentric argument, was both understandable and reversible. If contemporary Greeks were more like the Ottomans than other Europeans, it was because, unlike the latter, they had experienced neither the Renaissance nor the Enlightenment. They were kept by the Turks in the Middle Ages, as in museum. To catch up with the rest of Europe and to become what they were meant to be—"modern and civilized"—contemporary Greeks had to de-Ottomanize themselves, beginning with their language, which was to be purged of all foreign elements. Significantly, the language invented to replace the vernacular was called *katharevousa*, meaning "pure" or purified, and closely resembled ancient Greek. An indication of the power of this nationalist ideology is that this fictive language was still taught in schools in Greece and Cyprus as late as the 1960s.

It is within this context that the Greek Cypriot desire to unify Cyprus with Greece should be understood—a context in which it was asserted that by right, as descendants of the ancient Greeks, contemporary Greeks were de facto Europeans, even if not yet "modern and civilized." This is not to say that this claim went uncontested. But if it was possible to contest it in relation to mainland Greeks, it was even easier and more likely to do so with regard to Greek Cypriots. The island is much closer to Turkey and Syria than any part of Greece. The British and other European travelers expected its culture to be Levantine and, as we have seen, Durrell found the similarity of urban life in Cyprus to that of European cities a "disturbing anomaly." But it was not simply that Cyprus was thought of as part of the Middle East. It was also that the Cypriot claim to Greek ethnic identity was actively disputed by the British who wanted to maintain control of the island.[10] Becoming part of

Greece then was imperative. It would put an end to this sort of disputation and guarantee Cyprus' European credentials.

The Greek Cypriot call for union with Greece was met by the Turkish Cypriot call for the division of the island and union of one part with Turkey. Safety was no doubt paramount in this, but nationalist sentiments and their relation to cultural concerns should not be overlooked. Turkish Cypriots were themselves de-Ottomanizing themselves—a process of Europeanization initiated in mainland Turkey by Mustafa Kemal and the founding of the Turkish Republic in 1923. The Turks were determined to show the world (and themselves) that a Muslim country could be secular, democratic, modern, and civilized. They still are of course. In the last few decades, the aim has been to demonstrate that a Muslim country can be religious rather than secular and democratic, modern, and civilized. Indeed, given its history and proximity to Europe, it could also be a member of the European Union. Turkish Cypriots were warm supporters of the Kemalist revolution and its Europeanizing message and still are today, more so now perhaps than ever before. They too have been travelling in the West—on a different path perhaps but parallel to the Greek Cypriot path.

In 1960, Cyprus became an independent country despite itself but the seeds of conflict had already been sown and the first intercommunal violence erupted in 1963 to be followed by more violence in 1967.[11] In 1974, there was a coup against the then-president, Makarios, orchestrated by Greek Cypriot nationalists and Greek army officers stationed on the island the avowed aim of which was to unify Cyprus with Greece. A week later, Turkish troops invaded and occupied the northern part of the island. Greek Cypriots living in the north fled to the south and Turkish Cypriots living in the south moved to the north. A small opening in the dividing wall appeared in 2003 when the Turks decided to allow Greek Cypriots to visit their homes and properties in the north. In the same year, a United Nations-sponsored plan for the reunification of the island was put to the vote in both communities. Greek Cypriots overwhelmingly rejected it while Turkish Cypriots endorsed it by a large margin. The dispute remains unresolved and the country is still divided despite repeated efforts.

In 2004, Cyprus became a member of the European Union and, although officially it was the whole island that acceded, in practice the Acquis Communautaire could only be enforced in the area controlled by the internationally recognized (Greek Cypriot) government in the south. The accession was a momentous event and for many confirmed that Cyprus, much like Greece 23 years earlier, had finally achieved what it had always wanted to achieve—full recognition of its status as a European hence also "modern and civilized" society. It may have been travelling in the West, one could say, but not aimlessly and for nothing. The EU accession meant that it had finally arrived. But has it? It is certainly closer to Europe than it has even been, entangled in all sorts of institutions, legislation, bureaucratic networks, and the like. Yet, is closer ever close enough?[12] Can it ever be? I have suggested above that it cannot be if by "close enough" we mean identical. Europe needs non-Europe to be itself and its center needs a periphery if it is to be center.

The division between the European center and the periphery need not always be visible. Indeed, as we shall see shortly, because it is more often than not invisible, some mistakenly assume that it does not exist. But this is an illusion. As Durkheim rightly pointed out long ago, we feel the force of social facts only when we run up against them. The recent financial crisis constitutes a prime example of this. Most peripheral European societies crashed against the wall of this divide and were badly bruised, more so than anyone else perhaps Cyprus. Unlike other peripheral, liminal countries collectively and only half jokingly known as PIGS—Portugal, Italy, Greece and Spain—or PIIGS with the addition of Ireland in the mix, Cyprus is far too small to matter. It could therefore be punished and made an example of for others to heed without danger. Here is how the *Guardian* put the matter:

> Never before have bank account holders seen their savings raided to help finance a bailout.... Never before has Germany appeared so determined to make example of a Eurozone country, all the way to the euro exit, unless it does what it is told.... It is the Eurozone's fifth bailout in three years. But this time it is different. Since the beginning of the year, Berlin has been insisting that Cyprus is not "systemic", in other words that a Cypriot crash could be contained, with minimal impact on the rest of the Eurozone.[13]

We shall examine the moral economy of this punishment in due course. For the moment, I turn to the story of the "haircut" itself.

THE "HAIRCUT"

In the summer of 2012, it became apparent that the second largest Cypriot bank, Laiki Bank, which had been nationalized due to liquidity problems, required an extra €1.8 billion in recapitalization to remain solvent. Much like the other major Cypriot bank, the Bank of Cyprus, it had invested heavily in Greek government bonds and had lost large amounts of money. By this time the international credit agencies had downgraded Cyprus' rating to junk status, which meant that the money required could not be raised directly from the money markets. The Cypriot government therefore had no option but to ask the EU for financial assistance. Negotiations with the so-called Troika (European Commission, European Central Bank, and the International Monetary Fund) begun in earnest but dragged on largely because the communist government at the time had hopes of securing another loan from

Russia, as it had done two years earlier, hence avoiding the harsh conditions that the Troika was expected to impose.

In February 2013, there were elections in Cyprus and the new conservative government sought to speed up the negotiations. The expectation was that the Troika would be more positively inclined towards the country and its financial problems because, unlike the communists, the new government was clearly pro-European and pro-western and the new president, Anastassiades, maintained friendly relations with the leaders of major European countries, notably the German Chancellor, Angela Merkel. By this time, the amount of money needed to recapitalize the banks rose considerably. What is more, the new government as well as those who expected preferential treatment were in for a nasty surprise. At a meeting of the finance ministers of the Eurozone countries in Brussels, it was decided—under the guidance of the German finance minister and the strong support of the French, the Dutch, and the Finns— that any bail-out loan—now estimated in the region €10 billion—would have to be combined with a bail-in, meaning that a large part of the Cypriot banks' recapitalization would have to come from their customers' deposits. The Troika called this euphemistically a "tax," a one-off charge to help the banks stay afloat, but its significance was not lost on anyone. Without the depositors' trust, there can be no banks, and it was clear that in the case of Cyprus this trust was tested to the limit. The Cypriot delegation and the president, in particular, resisted the proposal because, as they rightly pointed out, it was bound to destroy the country's banking sector. Negotiations dragged into the night and finally, under extreme pressure, the president relented and accepted the package.

The deal was subject to ratification by the Cypriot parliament, which rejected it thus forcing the president to renegotiate. Under the new agreement, only deposits over €100,000 would be taxed. As it turned out, after months of calculations and negotiations, the rate came to almost 50% of all deposits over the 100,000 mark. The new packaged included the following: the closure of the second largest bank; the implementation of anti-money-laundering measures; fiscal consolidation to bring down the government budget deficit; structural reforms, primarily in the public sector; and an extensive privatization program. I shall not be concerned here with these measures. I will focus exclusively on the bail-in and explore in turn how EU officials justified it as well as the counterarguments put forward by the Cypriot side.

Before I turn to these arguments however, it may useful to refer briefly to how Turkish Cypriots received the news and reacted to this state of affairs. As I have already mentioned, although Greek Cypriots voted against the UN unification plan for Cyprus in 2003 and Turkish Cypriots for it, it was the former who became part of the EU in 2004 not the latter. Understandably, Turkish Cypriots felt betrayed by Europe and many resented the prosperity of the south, which was seen as being partly the outcome of joining the EU. It should not come as a surprise, therefore, that the news of the "haircut" was received with glee by Turkish Cypriot nationalist circles. As far as they were concerned, the "haircut" was a punishment that Greek Cypriots thoroughly deserved. For many others, however, who had jobs in the south or depended on Greek Cypriot clientele, such as the Turkish Cypriot casinos in the north, the crisis looked more ominous. For still others, it presented a unique opportunity for the reunification of the island. Some reasoned that a poorer Greek Cypriot side would be more willing to compromise. Others thought it was possible that Greek Cypriots would be tempted to presell part of the gas reserves recently discovered off the south coast of the island. As these reserves belonged equally to Turkish Cypriots, it would force Greek Cypriots to negotiate with Turkish Cypriots including perhaps an overall agreement for the settlement of the Cyprus problems itself. In the end, there was no need to presell any gas but there is little doubt that the woes of the Greek Cypriot economy affected the Turkish Cypriots as well. Many working in the south, mainly in the construction industry, lost their jobs as this sector of the economy was particularly badly hit by the crisis.

But to return to how EU officials presented the package of measures imposed on the Greek Cypriot economy, let me first turn to the statement made by Jörg Asmussen, a member of the executive committee of the European Central Bank, at the Economic and Monetary Affairs Committee of the European Parliament:

> In the 2000s, the Cypriot economy evolved towards a rather unbalanced business model with an inordinate weight for the financial industry. The country aimed to become leading provider [*sic*] of banking services. Cypriot banks attracted large inflows of foreign deposits.... The overall banking system represented more than 700% of the GDP ... An *active* use of the relevant policy tools could—and indeed should—have curbed these unsustainable developments. But *prudential* supervision was too *weak* and did not prevent the build-up of large financial sector imbalances [emphases added].[14]

I have highlighted the terms "active," "prudential," and "weak" because I wish to revisit them. For the moment let us turn to the German finance minister and a more blunt statement made just before the second Eurozone meeting in March. "The banking sector in Cyprus simply has no future in its current form. Everyone in the Euro-group agreed on this. The Cypriots' hope they could continue like this, attracting capital with low taxes and lax regulation and then others should pay for it when the model doesn't work any more—this is unfortunately an illusion and the ones in charge should explain this to their population."[15] There is a new element in this statement—lax regulation. While Asmussen simply said that the Cypriot "business model" was unbalanced and unsustainable because the banks were allowed to become too big for the size of the country, the German finance minister adds here that the banks became so big with money whose provenance was not properly checked. What he meant, of course, was money laundering, a widespread and persistent accusation among certain Eurozone countries, and, as we have seen, the target of one of the conditions of the Troika—the obligation imposed on the Cypriot government to allow independent auditors to carry out an investigation of banking practices in the country. Finally, let us note here the French finance minister's description of Cyprus as a "casino economy," an expression worthy of further comment, since there are no casinos in the south of the island and could not have meant "an economy based on casinos." It would be interesting then, to speculate on what the French finance minister meant.

The Cypriot counterargument was that the "business model" adopted by Cyprus and deemed unsustainable by the Troika was the very same model adopted by many other small countries, including European countries. Here is Christopher Pissarides, former London School of Economics Professor of Economics, Nobel Prize winner and currently Professor at the University of Cyprus and adviser to the President of Cyprus:

> The trouble, according to the troika, ... is that this [the measures taken by the Cypriot government after the Turkish invasion of 1974] also brought large amounts of large deposits to Cyprus, blowing up the banking sector to "unsustainable" dimensions. Deposits are about eight times the gross national product. This figure, however, is still smaller than Luxembourg's and not too different from that of Malta and Ireland.[16]

Moreover, as others pointed out, "the Cypriot business model is not something that they all discovered just now ['they,' meaning those who argued that it was unsustainable]. In a so-called convergence report dated 2007, one year before Cyprus joint the Eurozone, the ECB mentioned the large influx of capital"[17] —not disapprovingly, one presumes. As for the claim made by, among many others, the German finance minister, namely, that Cypriots could not expect others to come and pay for their failures, the Cypriot response was threefold: Firstly, it was pointed out that the EU and the Eurozone were built on the idea of solidarity among the member states. Cypriots were not shown this solidarity. To put the matter the way the German finance minister put it was to make a travesty of this idea. Secondly, this was not how other countries were rescued. Ireland and Spain, for example, faced similar problems to Cyprus and required a far larger amount of money to recapitalize their banks but no bail-in was imposed. Finally, the financial assistance given to Cyprus (as well as to the other countries "rescued") was not a gift. It was a loan expected to be fully repaid with interest.

There is finally the question of the money-laundering accusations. From the very beginning of the crisis, the Cypriot government responded to these allegations by pointing out that it had enacted strict anti-money-laundering regulations, ratifying international conventions and harmonizing domestic legislation with EU directives. But doubts continued to exist, particularly with regard to the implementation of these regulations and, as we have seen, the Cyprus government agreed to the Troika's demand for an independent audit. The report of this audit showed that, although there was room for improvement, the situation was not as bad as it had been presented. Indeed, as it turned out, the situation in Cyprus was far better than in the country that above any other had been accusing it of money laundering—Germany. The Cypriot press published reports of a Swiss nongovernmental organization (NGO), the Basel Institute on Governance, which showed that Cyprus was much lower than Germany on the list of money-laundering countries.

In the end, Cypriots explained the haircut in a rather predictable way—in terms of narrowly conceived economic interests and the power to impose one's will to serve those interests. Here is Pissarides again: "Cyprus finds that not all nations are equal. The interests of the Eurozone's large nations come first, says Christopher Pissarides."[18] This is the heading that the *Financial Times* used to introduce Pissarides's article already referred to and the essence of his argument. There are two problems with this way of understanding things, however. The first is the question of the interest of the large countries, and the second the "discovery" that European nations are not equal. To begin with, it is not clear how the interests of the large Eurozone countries such as Germany are served through the downsizing of the Cypriot banking sector. That some of the foreign money in Cypriot banks could move to these countries is quite possible. But it would be absurd to claim that this was the motive behind the German and French demands as the amount of money was far too small to have any impact on such large economies. Secondly, it is hard to believe that Cyprus or Pissarides speaking to the *Financial Times* on its behalf had only just now, in the midst of the crisis, found out that not all nations are equal. Everyone knows this and knows it quite well. Some nations in the EU—those of the northwest—are more equal than others—the eastern European nations, for example, and certainly the nations of southern Europe.

Take a country like Spain, a member of the stigmatized PIGS or PIIGS group. As Marion Fourcade argues in a discussion of the moral categories in the financial crisis, "the moral sinkhole has fuelled centrifugal tendencies as people and governments have been striving to distance themselves from those countries not (really) like them. Spain's desperate efforts to avoid a European stability mechanism/IMF program is all about the stigma of being lumped together in the same category as Greece."[19] Spain, it seems, did not wish to be part of the PIGS and to share in whatever comfort there might be in knowing that "we" are not the only ones. It knows full well that there is no equality in the union and wishes to be regarded as part of the more equal countries rather than the less equal. All southern and eastern European countries know this. This is the main, if not the only, reason they sought to become members of the EU to begin with. This is also why, with some exceptions perhaps, they are its most enthusiastic supporters. They wished to be among the "superior" countries at the center of the world, the very definition of what it means to be "modern and civilized." And let us be clear that it is not with economic equality we are concerned here. It is what it signifies—moral or, as anthropologists say, cultural equality. This is the core working hypothesis of this article: The economic is never divorced from the moral and the cultural, and the attempts of the Troika to present their "rescue" packages of southern European countries as the embodiment of economic rationality notwithstanding.

How then is the Cypriot "haircut" to be understood? There is no doubt that Cypriots have been punished for something and made an example of for other Eurozone countries to heed. But this punishment would be more fruitfully understood not within the context of taking—that is, serving narrowly conceived economic interests—but rather in the context of giving—giving light, therefore enlightening, those who are supposed not to have it and do not see clearly enough. This, let us remind ourselves, was the very rationale of the colonial enterprise and, although this enterprise has long ended, it would be a grave mistake to assume that imperialism itself has ended with it or that it is meant only for non-European countries. It is alive and well and in tune with the times—a "postmodern imperialism," as it has been called by a leading light[20]—both within and without. My claim then is that Cyprus has been punished and made an example for others to heed because in the eyes of countries like Germany and France it had not learned what it was supposed to know, namely, how to think and act as a proper, modern European society. The punishment was largely a civilizational lesson.

THE MORAL ECONOMY

In an article on the crisis and its moral aspects, Fourcade captures quite graphically the civilizational aspects of the financial assistance that countries receive in times of crisis from international bodies such as the IMF, and I will quote her here at some length. The assistance is "conditional," a "mix of coercion and training," she says. As such:

> It is a deeply corrective mechanism with inescapable moral effects. Aimed at governments, programmes have an unmistakable civilizational purpose—...to train, educate and profoundly reform those societies

whose poor performance has exposed them as inadequate, insufficient, incompetent and shackled by outdated institutions inimical to the flourishing of capitalism. Experts ... have their own vocabulary to designate the typical flaws: rampant "corruption", low "state capacity", poor "governance", "rigidities" of all sorts and "inefficient" policies.[21]

It should not come as a surprise that this was also the terminology used by the "experts" to describe the Cypriot case. Here is a quote from the *Guardian* again.

> Angela Merkel, the German chancellor, takes the view that the Cypriot financial and economic model is *rotten to the core*, needs *vital overhauling* if it is to be saved and that Germany is not going to send its taxpayers' money to secure the low-tax, high-risk investments of Russian squillionaires dominating the *bloated* Cypriot financial sector [emphases added].[22]

Let us also remind ourselves here how Asmussen describes the Cypriot economy in his address to the Economic and Monetary Affairs Committee of the European Parliament. Asmussen says that, although the Cypriot government had at its disposal all the relevant policy tools to curb the "unsustainable" development of the banking sector, it did not make "active" use of them; although there was some kind of supervision of the banks, this was "too weak." In effect, he says what Fourcade says that the experts say about countries in such cases—limited "state capacity," poor "governance," and the like. In fact, he is saying far more than that or, at any rate, he is saying things that point to historical connections between economy and culture as well as culture and power. It is *prudential* supervision that was "too weak" in Cyprus, Asmussen says. This term—prudential—is not at all innocent. It carries tremendous cultural baggage that we need to investigate.

Prudence comes from the Latin *prudentia*, which is a contraction of providentia, meaning foresight. The Oxford dictionary defines prudence as being sensible and careful when you make judgements and decisions, in effect avoiding unnecessary risks.[23] However, a better definition is that of the Merriam-Webster dictionary—prudence: the ability to govern and discipline oneself by the use of reason.[24] This definition is better for two reasons. Firstly, it explains why people lack foresight and are not being careful and sensible when they make judgements and decisions, in short, why they take unnecessary risks. It is because their reason cannot control and discipline their desires and passions—this being the stereotype of Mediterranean people as warm blooded and impulsive. The Merriam-Webster definition is better than the Oxford definition also because it allows us to see the cultural baggage that the term carries with it as well as to make historical connections. This tenet—the ability to govern and discipline oneself by using one's reason—is the criterion used to make and justify a whole host of divisions. This is how European men saw themselves over the last few centuries—as being in possession of the ability to master nature within—the archetype being perhaps the Victorian male. It is how European men legitimized divisions and power relations within—patriarchy, for example—as much as divisions and power relations without—I am thinking here of the colonial enterprise itself. The image of the natives in the colonial literature as being innocent like children who do not know any better and cannot be allowed to run their own lives without instruction and close supervision is well known to anthropologists to require elaboration here.

I am not suggesting of course that in using the term "prudential" Rasmussen meant to say that Cypriots could not use their reason to discipline themselves and to control their desires. For all we know, he may not even have written the speech himself. Yet, it is not personal intention that counts here but cultural history inscribed in language. In this sense, the civilizing, modernizing, Europeanizing implications of what has been said are unmistakable. Cypriots should have known better than to allow their banking sector to grow to eight times the gross national product (GNP). They should have been able to foresee the danger and to realize that they were taking an unacceptable risk. But perhaps, being a Mediterranean people, they became too enthusiastic about turning their country into a center for international banking and were carried away by the excitement. Taking unacceptable risks is also what the French finance minister may have meant in describing Cyprus as a "casino economy." Gambling means placing your faith for gain in nothing more than blind fate. This apparently is the reverse of economic rationality.

Let us finally turn to the question of the interests of the big countries, which as Pissarides says always come first. We have already noted that it is not inaccurate to say this. What is problematic, rather, is the assumption, firstly, that these interests are always material and, secondly, that they are always served by taking, as Pissarides implies in the case of Germany versus Cyprus. If the big countries can destroy the banking sector of small countries like Cyprus, their financial industries have much to gain. Let us remind ourselves that this is exactly what happened many times over during the colonial era, for example, Britain destroying India's textile industry in order to promote its own. Yet, colonial and imperialist thinking in general demonstrate *also* that the best way to serve one's interests is not by taking but, paradoxically, by giving. This is so because, as Derrida argues so compellingly in his analysis of Marcel Mauss's book on the gift, giving is taking with a certain capitalization or interest.[25] This is not because the gift is repaid by the countergift of the recipient. The interest is virtually instantaneous. As soon as one thinks about making a gift to someone else, one is instantly repaid with interest. The return is not anything material but it is a profit nonetheless, for example, the pleasure in knowing that one's gift will make someone else happy or in knowing that one is doing the right thing. Serving one's interests is not something that one can avoid. If there were no interest to be gained in giving a gift, there would be no interest in giving it.

Elsewhere, I reflected on this paradox of taking by means of giving with the help of Kipling's famous poem "The White Man's Burden."[26] As the poem says, the white man shouldered this burden—sent his "sons to exile," asked them to "wait in heavy harness" and to "seek another's profit" and so on—knowing too well through experience that the only reward he will ever receive from the natives is "the blame of those ye better, the hate of those ye guard."[27] The white man gives the light of civilization to the rest of the world and receives nothing in return or worse, blame and hatred. He sacrifices himself for nothing and insists on continuing to do so. Is the white man a saint or a fool? He is neither of course. It really does not matter that he receives no countergift from the natives, say, gratitude. He has already been repaid with an interest. He has done the most "profitable" thing—giving—and reaped the most "valuable reward," as Winston Churchill once put it:

> What enterprise that an *enlightened* community may attempt is more *noble* and more *profitable* than the reclamation from *barbarism* of fertile regions and large populations? To *give* peace to warring tribes, to administer justice where all was violence, to strike the chains off the slave, to draw the richness from the soil, to plant the earliest seeds of commerce and learning, to increase in whole peoples their capacities for pleasure and diminish their chances for pain—what more *beautiful ideal* or more valuable *reward* can inspire human effort [emphases added]?[28]

The most valuable reward is precisely the confirmation of the "enlightened community" as such a community—enlightened, civilized, and, of course, superior to the "barbarian populations" to which it gives.

I believe this is the context in which we should place and try to understand Germany's determination to punish Cyprus and to make it an example for other countries in the south and the east to heed—a neocolonial or postmodern imperialist context. Germany punished Cyprus not out of vindictiveness but for the island's own good, not to serve its economic interests but to discipline and teach Cyprus a lesson—a civilizational lesson. Can there be anything more profitable?

NOTES

1. Amitav Ghosh, *In an Antique Land* (London: Granta Publications, 1992).
2. Edward Said, *Orientalism* (New York: Vintage Books, 1979).
3. A number of writers have argued that modernity is itself liminal; see, in particular, Arpad Szakolczai, *Reflexive Historical Sociology* (London: Routledge, 2000); and Agnes Horvath, Bjørn Thomassen, and

Harald Wydra, eds., *Breaking Boundaries: Varieties of Liminality* (New York: Berghahn Books, 2015). This is not very different from my claim that it is nothing or, at any rate, a figment of the imagination. To be liminal is to be neither here nor there but everywhere, hence nowhere (in particular), neither this nor that hence nothing.

4. Michael Herzfeld, *Anthropology Through the Looking-Glass: Critical Ethnography in the Margins of Europe* (Cambridge: Cambridge University Press, 1987).

5. Lawrence Durrell, *Bitter Lemons of Cyprus* (London: Faber and Faber, 1959), 34.

6. Dipesh Chakrabrty, *Provincializing Europe* (Princeton: Princeton University Press, 2000).

7. Catholic Northern Ireland could perhaps be said to be another such case.

8. See Michael Herzfeld, *Anthropology Through the Looking-Glass*, and Martin Bernal, *Black Athena: The Afroasiatic Roots of Classical Civilization, Vol. 1: The Fabrication of Ancient Greece 1785–1985* (New Brunswick, NJ: Rutgers University Press, 1987).

9. Benedict Anderson, *Imagined Communities* (London: Verso, 1991).

10. George Hill, *A History of Cyprus*, Vol. IV (Cambridge: At the University Press, 1952)

11. The literature on the ethnic conflict in Cyprus is vast and I cannot do it justice. I can refer here only to a few notable anthropological examples: Yiannis Papadakis, *Echoes from the Dead Zone: Across the Cyprus Divide* (London: I. B. Tauris, 2005); Rebecca Bryant, *Imagining the Modern: The Cultures of Nationalism in Cyprus* (London: I. B. Tauris, 2004); Lisa Dikomitis, *Cyprus and its Places of Desire: Cultures of Displacement among Greek and Turkish Cypriot Refugees*, London: I. B. Tauris, 2012); and Yael Navarro-Yashin, *The Make-Believe Space: Affective Geography in a Postwar Polity* (Durham, NC: Duke University Press, 2012).

12. See Vassos Argyrou, "Is 'Closer and Closer' Ever Close Enough? De-Reification, Diacritical Power and the Specter of Evolutionism," *Anthropological Quarterly* 69(4): 206–219 (1996).

13. Ian Traynor, "This Time Is Different: Euro Exit Could Be Cyprus's Only Way Out," *The Guardian*, (24 March 2013), www.theguardian.com/world/2013/mar/24/germany-stands-firm-over-cyprus (accessed 1 Aug. 2016).

14. Jorg Asmussen, "Exchange of Views with the Economic and Monetary Affairs Committee of the European Parliament on Fiscal Assistance to Cyprus: Introductory Remarks" (March 2013), www.europa.eu/press/key/date/2013/html/sp130508.en.html (accessed 1 Aug. 2016).

15. Quoted in Valentina Pop, "Cyprus 'Business Model' Was No Mystery to the EU" (March 2013), htpps://euobserver.com/institutional/119531. (accessed 1 Aug. 2016)

16. Christopher Pissarides, "Cyprus Finds Not All Nations Are Equal" (March 2013), www.ft.com/content/e109906e-9718-11e2-8950-00144feabdc0. (accessed 1 Aug. 2016)

17. Pop, "Cyprus 'Business Model.'"

18. Pissarides, "Cyprus Finds."

19. Marion Foucarde, "The Economy as Morality Play, and Implications for the Eurozone Crisis," *Socio-Economic Review* 11: 620–27 (2013). For a different take on Greece's financial problems, see Michael Herzfeld, "The Hypocrisy of European Moralism: Greece and the Politics of Cultural Aggression," *Anthropology Today* 32(2): 10–13 (2016).

20. Robert Cooper, *The Postmodern State and the World Order* (Demos, n.d.).

21. Foucarde, "The Economy as Morality."

22. Traynor, "This Time."

23. https://en.oxforddictionaries.com/definition/prudence (accessed 1 Aug. 2016)

24. https://www.merriam-webster.com/dictionary/prudence (accessed 1 Aug. 2016)

25. See Jacques Derrida, *Given Time: 1. Counterfeit Money* (Chicago: The University of Chicago Press, 1994).

26. Vassos Argyrou, *The Gift of European Thought and the Cost of Living* (New York: Berghahn Books, 2013).

27. Quoted in Niall Ferguson, *Empire: How Britain Made the Modern World* (London: Penguin Books, 2004), xxvii.

28. Rudyard Kipling, "The white man's burden" (1899), http://www.kiplingsociety.co.uk/poems_burden.htm (accessed 1 Aug. 2016)

Index

Note: **Boldface** page numbers refer to tables and *italic* page numbers refer to figures. Page numbers followed by "n" denote endnotes.

Ahrweiler, Helene 86
Alexandrescu, Sorin 53
Anglo-Irish Agreement 108
annexation of Crimea 79n14
antagonism 104, 106, 109; in Northern Ireland 112
Archangelism 45, 47
Arendt, Hannah 98–9
Asmussen, Jörg 125
asymmetric federalism 92

Baltic States, collapse of Soviet Union 71
Banac, Ivo 89
Bank of Cyprus 123
Bateson, Gregory 4–5, 7, 16n11, 85
"Bateson's Rule" 8
Bauman, Zygmunt 53
Bayly, C. A. 89
Becali, George 54
Beck, Ulrich 61
Belfast City Council 114
Belting, Hans 72
Bessarabia 35–6; Bessarabian society 39; Inochentists 42; Julian calendar 35; monastic institutions 35; Romanian Orthodox church 35
Birth of the Modern World 1780–1914, The (Bayly) 89
Bitter Lemons of Cyprus (Durrell) 119
Blaga, Lucian 54
Bloodlands, the (Snyder) 102
Boia, Lucian 55
Bon, Gustave le 7
Book of Ezra 3
Bosnia and Herzegovina (B&H) 82, 83; identity 91; postconflict selfhood in 91; social-habitus in 86

Breuilly, John 84
British government 101, 107, 108, 112
British–Irish affairs 109
British–Irish Council 111
Brubaker's concept 20
brutality of imperial war 99
Byzantine Empire 85–6

Carpathian Basin 22
Central-Eastern Europe 65–6; ambivalence and mutability 69; centralized marginality, notion of 77; ethnic minorities 67, 71–4; geopolitical developments 78; liminality in politics, human side of 69–71, 77; as marginal center 68–9; multiple paradoxes 79n17; national narratives 69; religious experience 72; scapegoating mechanisms 67, 68, 74, 76; victimhood-based identity 67, 74–7
charismatic Judaism 37 *see also* Judaism
civilizing process 12, 86
"collective representations" concept 5
concupiscential conquest 3
conflict management 92–3
consociationalism 92
contemporary politicians 85
Crainic, Nichifor 54
"crisis within a crisis" 100
Culeac, Alexandru 44–6; Archangelism 45, 47; *Vision That Appeared in the Year 1920* 45
Cyprus 119; anti-money-laundering regulations 127; business model 125–6; casino economy 126, 130; colonial rule 120; economic interests 127, 128; elections 124; European Union 122; financial and economic model 129; gross national product 130; intercommunal violence 122; *katharevousa* language 121; Laiki Bank recapitalization 123; nationalism 120; prudence 129; state capacity 129; taxation 124; troika system 123–4, 126; unsustainable development 129

INDEX

Dâncu, Vasile 55
Dayton Peace Agreement (DPA) 84
decolonization 106
Deletant, Dennis 55
depersonalization 2; minority person *vs.* 3–5; negative aspects of 4
Djuvara, Neagu 55
Donetsk National Republic 77
DPA *see* Dayton Peace Agreement
dual citizenship *see* Hungarian dual citizenship
Dumouchel, Paul 103, 104
Durkheim, Emile 5
Durrell, Lawrence 119–20

Eastern Roman Empire 12
egocentrism 91
Eliade, Mircea 60
Elias, Norbert 82, 86
Elijah 34, 37–8, 42, 44–5
Eminescu, Mihail 54
empire-building 3, 12
empire loyalists 104, 105
End of Days 38–40, 42, 44, 47
Enoch 37–8, 42, 44, 45
Equality Commission 111
ethnic frontier 99, 104–6
ethnicity 8
ethnic minorities 2, 54, 66, 67, 78; as metareality 71–4
ethnocentrism: Hungarian minorities 24; in Transylvania 23
ethnozenship 22
European Central Bank 125
European Economic Community 106
Europeanization 121, 122
European Union 70, 122; Cyprus 119, 122; financial assistance 123

Fico, Robert 28
First World War 35, 68–9
Foucault, Michel 3
French Revolution 121
Funar, Gheorghe 54

Gaelic Athletic Association 112
General Economic History 4
Germany: money laundering 127; taxpayers' money 129
GFA *see* Good Friday Agreement
Gherman, Sabin 55
Ghosh, Amitav 118
Girard, René 7, 72, 102, 114; mimetic desire, concept of 82; sacrificial mechanisms 68, 82; victimhood theory 67
Gnosticism 60, 87
Good Friday Agreement (GFA)110–12, 115
Great Schism 5

Greece: civilization 121; Cypriot economy 125; financial and economic model 129; independence 121; Ottoman province 121
Guelke, Adrian 87, 91

Habermas-Rawlsian political philosophy 14
Habsburg Monarchy 9
Hennis, Wilhelm 4, 15n3
Home Rule 100–1
homogeneity, Hungarian citizenship 27
Horvath, Agnes 59
Hungarian dual citizenship 19–20; Brubaker's concept 20; Carpathian Basin 22; citizenship 19–22; elements of identity **25**; elements of minority 19; ethnic identity 19; ethnocentrism 23, 24; everyday life 26; homeland 21; homogeneity 27; liminality 30; liminoid accessibility 23; minority ethnocentrism 24; minority identities 24–7; passport 25; referendum 29; regional identity 21; in Slovakia 28; in Subcarpathia 21; territory-based 26; trickster logic 29–30; Ukraine 21; verbal communication 28; xenophobia 29
Hungarian–Hungarian boundary-making 23
Hungarian–Hungarian relations 24, 26
Husserl, Edmund 57

IFI *see* International Fund for Ireland
imitation 2, 5, 7, 10
Inalcik, Halil 89
Independent Commission on Policing 111
Inochentie *43*, 44–6; Balta 39; charismatic healing ministry 40; "harmful influence" 40; Inochentism 42, 47; religious revival of 39; spiritual distress 40
Inochentism 34, 39, 42, 47
Inochentist movement *41*
International Fund for Ireland (IFI) 109
Iohannis, Klaus 56
Ionescu, Nae 54
Ireland: crisis of nationality in 100–2; government 107; Home Rule parliament in 101; imperial state failed in 100; peace process 108–10; Republican Army killings 112; self-determination 108, 110; *see also* Northern Ireland
Irish Free State 105
Irish Parliamentary Party 101
Itzkowitz, N. 90

Judaism 37, 38
Julian calendar 35
Jung, C. G. 83
Jungian process 91–2

Kaczyński, Lech 73
Kant, Immanuel 13, 82, 87

INDEX

Karnoouh, Claude 55
katharevousa language 121
Kemalist revolution 122
Kemal, Mustafa 122
Kideckel, David 55
kin-state 8; minority community 10–11; politicians 10
Kligman, Gail 55

Laiki Bank recapitalization 123
legitimacy 98–100
legitimate violence, monopoly of 98
Levitzki, Feodosie 40
Levizor, Ioan *see* Inochentie
Liiceanu, Gabriel 55
liminality 2, 5–6, 14, 15, 16n8, 34, 47, 84–5; in politics, human side of 69–71, 77; umbrella of 86
"liminal" Orthodoxy 37, 47
liquid modernity 53
Löfgren, Orvar 58
Luhansk National Republic 77

Makarios 122
"marginality/liminality" 2
MASSR *see* Moldovan Autonomous Soviet Socialist Republic
Mauss, Marcel 5, 29
Members of the Legislative Assembly (MLAs) 111
Merkel, Angela 124, 129
Michael 34, 38, 44–6
millet system 88–90
mimetic desire, concept of 82
minorities 1–2; ethnocentrism 24; existence 9, 11–15; presence of 8
minority identities, Hungarian dual citizenship 19, 25; and citizenship identity 24; elements of **25**, 27; patterns 24, 27; territory-based 25, 26
minority person: daily life of 9; depersonalization *vs.* 3–5; dialogue of 9; kin-state politicians and 10; life strategies 9–10; perceived closeness of 11
MLAs *see* Members of the Legislative Assembly
"modernization" projects 13
"Moldavian Lourdes" 40
Moldovan Autonomous Soviet Socialist Republic (MASSR) 36
Moldovan Orthodox church 34
Moldovan Soviet Socialist Republic 36
money laundering 126, 127
monopoly, of legitimate violence 98
Morgenthau, Hans 59

nationalism: certain form of 81; conflict handling 92–3; gestures of 88; mimetic violence of 82; Ottomans' millets system 88–90; postcommunist and postconflict democratization 90–1; quasi-unifying 86; social ideology of 82; trickster 82–5
nationalizing state 8, 19
national self-determination 99, 103, 108, 112, 115
natural attitude 56, 57
Nica, Antim 43
Nicholas, Tsar 39
Nietzsche, Friedrich Wilhelm 3, 4, 7
nihilism 4
Noica, Constantin 54
North Atlantic Treaty Organization (NATO) 70
Northern Ireland: administration 113; antagonism in 112; controlling dynamic of 111; decisive challenges in 112; direct confrontation with 107; government 107; Home Rule parliaments in 101; internal affairs 113; in 1940s 106; politics 107; power-sharing in 110; recalcitrant antagonists 111; of reconciliation 115; self-determination in 109; truce/transformation 112–14; violence in 106
North-South cooperation 110
Novorossiya (New Russia) 76, 77, 80n39

Orban, Viktor 28
Ottoman Empire 88, 89, 99
Ottomans' millets system 88–90
"out-of-ordinary" *(ausseralltägliche)* situation 6
"overseas", concept of 99

"paradox of belonging" 53
Partidul Democrat (PD) 56
Partidul Național Liberal (PNL) 55–6
Partidul Național Țărănesc–Creștin Democrat (PNȚCD) 55
Partidul Social Democrat (PSD) 55–6
Partidul Socialist al Muncii (PSM) 56
Patapievici, Horia Roman 55
peace process 108–10
peace treaty 13, 82, 83, 93
"perestroika" 90
permanent liminality 82, 84, 85
perpetual peace treaty 13, 82, 94n5
Pissarides, Christopher 126, 127
Pizzorno, Alessandro 79n25
Pleșu, Andrei 55
Polish-Lithuanian relations 73
political accommodation 92
political anthropology 2–3
political sociology 6
political violence 103
Politics as a Vocation 5
Ponta, Victor 56
Popovschi, Nicolai 39, 42
post-Revolutionary France 75
postwar liberal democracy 109
Prevention of Terrorism Act 108

135

INDEX

Pridnestrovian Moldavian Republic 36
Protestant community 105
Protestant Ethic 4
prudence 129
public sphere 4
Puric, Dan 54

quasi-unifying nationalism 86

Radin, Paul 6, 16n9
recapitalization 123–4
reconciliation 108, 109; and nonviolence 110; Northern Ireland of 115; rivalry and 110–11; transcendence for 110
"religious war" 107
Republic of Moldova, religious movements in: Archangelism 45, 47; ethnic minority communities 35; Inochentism 34, 39, 42, 47; Moldovan Autonomous Soviet Socialist Republic 36; Moldovan Soviet Socialist Republic 36; Orthodoxy 34; religious aspects 34; territorial vulnerability 34
Ringmar, Erik 88
rite of passage 6, 84–6
Rites de passage 5
Romanian Orthodoxy 34, 35, 47
Romanian postcommunist nationalism 52–3; contemporary discourses of 52–6; epistemological paradox 56–8; essentialism and constructionism 54, 56, 63n4; matrix space context 54; media and academic life 53; modern nationalism 59–60; paradox of belonging 53; political discourses 55–6; principle of modernity 61; risk analysis, planning and 62; scientific and natural attitude 57; social reform 61
Romanian thinkers 54–5
Russian Orthodoxy 34–6, 40

sacrificial mechanisms 82
Sakwa, Richard 79n14
scapegoating mechanisms 67, 68, 74, 76
schismatic processes, unfolding of 8
schismogenesis 2, 5, 7, 15, 85, 87, 91
Schmitt, Carl 98
Schutz, Alfred 57
scientific attitude 57
scission 87
Second World War 43, 69
self-determination 99, 105, 115
self-referentiality 5
"Serbo-Croatian" language 83–4
Short Life and Deeds of Father Inochentie of Balta 39
Snyder, Timothy 102
social contract 102
social ideology of nation 82

social peace 102
social theory 5
Southern Ireland, Home Rule parliaments in 101
"Soviet existence" 70
Sovietization 71
Soviet Union 9, 36; brutal modernization 70; collapse of 66; occupation, world wars and 68; post-Soviet condition 71, 74
Sovremennaya psikhiatriya (Yakovenko) 42
Stăniloae, Dumitru 54
"state of exception" 98
state territorial sovereignty 98
stilists 35
Syrian refugees 75
Szakolczai, Arpad 59, 82, 85
Székely population 75–6
Szekler National Council 76

Taleb, Nicholas 62
Tarde, Gabriel 5, 7, 94n2
territorial jurisdiction 100
"territorial larger forces" 101
territory 98–100
Tešan, Jesenko 13
Tocqueville, Alexis de 5, 12
transcendental deduction 87
transcendental idealism 92
transcendent order 102–3
transformation, in Northern Ireland 112–13
transgression of normality 83, 87
Transnistria 36, 43
Transylvanian identity 55
Transylvanian School (*Şcoala Ardeleană*) 60
Treaty of Westphalia 12
trickster 2, 5, 6–7, 10, 13, 15, 82–5; identity (de)formation 86–8
troika system 123
truce, in Northern Ireland 112–13
Trump, Donald 75
Tudor, Corneliu Vadim 54
Turkish Cypriot 122; de-Ottomanizing 122; Kemalist revolution 122
Turner, Victor 70
Ţuţea, Petre 54

Ukraine 70, 76, 78n11, 79n14
Union of Soviet Socialist Republics (USSR) 84
United Nations 122
U-turn process 83, 87, 93

van Gennep, Arnold 5, 70, 84
Verdery, Katherine 55
Vermes, Géza 37
victimhood-based identity 67, 74–7
"victims of violence" 108
Victorian democratic reforms 100

INDEX

violence 102–3; legitimacy for 106; monopoly of 109; in Northern Ireland 115
Visions of Grigore Culiac and his Sufferings for the Confession of the Second Coming of Jesus Christ, The (Grigore) 45
Vision That Appeared in the Year 1920, A (Alexandru) 45
Voegelin, Eric 3, 59, 60
Vojvodina 21, 22
Volksgeist, Herderian conception of 54

"war of attrition" 108
"War Treaties" 82
Weber, Max 3–6, 15, 15n4, 16n5, 57, 98
Western political system 98
Western Roman Empire 12
Wilson, Woodrow 99, 103
Wright, Frank 99, 100, 104, 105
Wydra, Harald 59

Yeltsin, Boris 70